Letters To A Young Man In Search Of Himself

Victor La Cerva, MD

Published By:
Heartsongs Publications
Santa Fe New Mexico

ISBN 978-0-9893905-2-1
Author Copyright © 2018
Victor La Cerva, MD
Book design by Joseph Woods

Printed in the United States of America

Publisher's Cataloging-In-Publication
(Provided by Cassidy Cataloguing Services Inc.)
Names:
La Cerva, Victor, author.
Title:
Letters to a young man in search of himself / Victor La Cerva.
Description:
Santa Fe, New Mexico : Heartsongs Publications, [2018] |
Audience: Young men, ages 20-40.
Identifiers:
ISBN: 978-0-9893905-2-1
Subjects:
LCSH: Men--Psychology. | Man-woman relationships. | Men--
Family relationships. | Fatherhood. | Personality and emotions.
| Self-actualization (Psychology) | Self-realization. | Interper-
sonal relations. | Spiritual life. | BISAC: SOCIAL SCIENCE
/ Men's Studies. | BODY, MIND & SPIRIT / Inspiration &
Personal Growth. | FAMILY & RELATIONSHIPS / General. |
SELF-HELP / Personal Growth / General. | SOCIAL SCIENCE
/ Gender Studies | PSYCHOLOGY / Interpersonal Relations.
Classification:
LCC: HQ1090 .L332 2018 | DDC: 305.31--dc23

DEDICATION & GRATITUDE

For my father, who continues to inspire me to be a kind, creative, generous man.

This book honors young men everywhere. May you discover your true essence, and develop your unique talents. The world is desperately in need of your gifts and service.

Especially for those who left us far too early: Bernie, Avi, Isaiah, Mario, Michael, and Caleb.

In addition to the men who offered words of praise, heartfelt thanks to these fine young men whose feedback kept me on a meaningful path: Nick Davis, Dylan Duncan, Chris Grimes, Chris Knight, Julian Marquez, Ian McMahon, James Muir, Jeremy Nurse, Micah Pearson, Jesse Voremberg, Nathan Waldman, and Chris Wismar,

Deep appreciation for Carla's intuitive wisdom and helpful, clarifying conversations.

Thanks to Jacob Brancasi for editing support.

Mille grazie to Joseph Woods, a fine artist, graphic artist and photographer.
Please visit www.josephandkris.com

WORDS OF PRAISE

Honest, poetic, thought-provoking, engaging, enlightening, intense book. Every sentence a bold encounter with oneself and what it means to be a young man searching in this world.
Maurice L Fleming, former homeless young man, now a youth counselor.

It felt like the Fatherhood Letter was a personal note written just for me. Extremely helpful and insightful at a time when I can use all the support I can get.
John Froehlich, new father, outdoor photographer and waiter.

Thoughtful and provocative. An earnest request to live with a capital "L", and to examine my own premises and assumptions. Both challenging and invigorating, without the preachy overtones one often finds in this genre. An invitation to go just a little bit deeper.
Michael Kaplan, bartender and fine woodworker.

A well written, insightful and experience-rigged rich collection of Letters. I especially appreciated new and different insights on Being Stuck and Habits & Intention. I am an avid reader and new and different has become a rare delicacy to be honored.
Allen Matsika, African immigrant and MBA student.

This book is a refreshingly bold and transparent work for men of all ages to explore their masculinity and femininity. It offers non-judgmental guidance to our boys in a time when it is most needed. My heart bursts with gratitude, joy and love when I read these letters.

Craig Thomas McAdams, actor, professor, psychotherapist and husband.

From what I have read, this book is amazing. Every time I settle in to read it, someone walks in or the phone rings. I really enjoy Victor's writing and can't wait to receive a printed copy.

Mike Lucero, Subaru mechanic, avid hunter and father of two girls.

A wonderful tool for understanding the true nature of yourself and how to navigate in the world. Discovering your life path, trusting your unique personality, and understanding the call of your spirit are admirable and difficult quests. Victor has called on his own insight and history to help find the way through the troubled waters of self discovery. A guidebook for all young men embarking on their own life quest.

Benjamin Bailey-Buhner, performer, writer, owner of The Bookman & The Lady.

In this easy to read book, Victor touches upon the basic areas of wisdom that are needed to create a rich and fulfilling life. For a young man who is seeking fulfillment, purpose, passion and wealth, this book is a helpful compass on the turbulent seas of life. Follow the alchemy that this book teaches and you will claim what your heart, mind and soul is looking for - and much much more!

Tyger White, programmer, artist and community leader.

A guide to self-exploration. Every line and chapter provide unique opportunities for reflection, healing, gender analysis, and growth. As a 24 year-old man motivated to understand masculinity more critically, I will be giving this book to all of my male friends.

Sean Wils, recent college graduate trying to find meaning and figure out life in New York City.

Wholesome, uplifting, inspiring, and encouraging exploration of the human elements that afford us wellbeing and happiness. Incisive descriptions of the dynamics underlying how we relate to the world with unique insights into ways of cultivating the strong, confident, creative, and capable people we're here to be. Beautiful map for anyone seeking balance and direction in navigating the mind, heart, and soul in alignment with the greatest good.

Jonathan Meade, Visual Director, All Aboard Earth.

CONTENTS

I Question everything		9
II Being a Man		17
III The Nature of the Journey		25
IV Parents		33
V Demystifying Emotions		41
VI Anger		49
VII Fear		57
VIII Sadness		65
IX Forgiveness		73
X Solitude and Friendship		81
XI Sexuality		89
XII Love		97
XIII Fatherhood		105
XIV Desire		113
XV Purpose		121
XVI Being Stuck		129
XVII Habits and Intention		137
XVIII Altered Consciousness		145
XIX Creativity		153
XX Happiness and Freedom		161
XXI Spirituality		169
Parting Thoughts		177

I

QUESTION EVERYTHING

Since the time before words, older men have passed on to younger ones their best wisdom through sharing both skills and stories. The natural intergenerational rhythms that once allowed younger men to regularly feel the vibrations of what manhood is really about – to apprentice or be mentored by an older caring man – are often lost in a haze of modern busyness. These letters are an attempt to bridge that gap in a small but meaningful way. I have lived a long and interesting life and had my share of engaging experiences, both uplifting and challenging. I have witnessed many births and deaths, and regularly seen the suffering all men carry deep inside. How am I not being my authentic self? Whose life is this anyway? I have struggled with these dilemmas, and often wallowed in a morass of disappointments at what I have created for myself. I have tasted truths unattainable by logic, pierced some of the great lies foisted by societal fears, and learned to embrace the Great Mystery.

I now know that change comes not from battling the old, but rather forging a new path that simply makes the old obsolete, because it is more satisfying.

I speak to that which is highest in you, to the part of you that is so happy to just be alive in this precious moment, and knows when the path you follow is of the heart. To the you who sees clearly the madness of humanity's present earth course, which keeps so many from connecting to what matters most—family, community, and the natural beauty and bounty of this amazing planet. It is easy to lose faith in human intelligence, even as one admires the resiliency and resourcefulness of our species.Human brains evolved in complex environments, nourished by dizzying arrays of diverse stimuli. So many unconscious, collective, cultural choices influence your life. I want you to create an inner revolution, to develop some new *thoughtstreams*. I speak to that which is highest in you, not as a wise sage but as a fellow traveler, searching, seeking, suffering, singing and dancing with it all, just as you.

Confused, bored, discouraged, apathetic, disorganized, overwhelmed, insecure or uncertain? Drink deeply from the well of what I call essential questions—vital queries that you must keep asking throughout your journey. By stimulating thought and intentionality, they help you to glimpse the life you are not yet ready to fully inhabit. I have definitely found that how consciously I am living my life is directly dependent on the essential questions I am holding.

They challenge assumptions, provoke awareness and generate the energy needed for change and further progress. You live along into the answers, which may keep changing as you grow.

Think of them as cairns, which help to keep you on the path.

They are meant to engage you in a way that makes hearing your own inner guidance more possible.

The riddles that beguile you are beautiful and worthy of your attention. Asking and holding questions allows your personal authentic truth – rather than a more general external axiom – to emerge.

Essential questions don't need an outright answer and often require a lifetime of pondering.

Because they arise from an existential thirst and demand that you expose yourself, they can serve as a chariot to carry you across the breadth of your life, and draw you to what you most need for your evolution.

Kneel down in praise of them! Sometimes, you are closer to the essence of who you really are when you are asking questions, than when you think you have all the answers.

What is the primary cause of your own suffering?

What habits and beliefs do you still cling to, that no longer serve you?

For what do you most need to forgive yourself?

Who are your heroes and why?

Who or what inspires you?

What would you be doing if you had no fear?

How do you honor yourself?

What is your own personal definition of success?

In what ways do you continue to deceive yourself?

Who comprises your Greek chorus?

Do you spend more time and energy trying to figure out the meaning of life, than you do experiencing the rapture of being alive?

What feelings flow when you gaze into your own eyes?

At this point on your journey, what are you most curious about?

What have you lost touch with that is very important to you?

I invite your curiosity, and you absolutely have the right to remain skeptical. Question everything until you discover what resonates as true. Along the way my intention is that you will explore the inner work of becoming a conscious, empowered man—what qualities of being to cultivate, and what obstacles to overcome. There is no brightly marked finish line when you are confirmed with a diploma that declares you are a real man. These letters will assist you to develop skills in various essential arenas of wellbeing. Read and revisit them at your leisure. Share and discuss them with friends. You will find your own relevant pearls of wisdom when you are ready to receive and live them. I hope the letters will inspire, provoke, enthrall, challenge, and illuminate rather than obfuscate.

Your real journey in life is interior. The answers to life's questions rest within, and all you need do is look, listen and trust. There are three aspects to living: the creative or that which you bring into existence, the experiential or what happens to you, and the attitudinal or your response to circumstances, including the difficult challenges, confrontations and calamities you inevitably will encounter. Your mind inherently has the potential and capacity for awareness.

Consciousness just is. It is an intrinsic property of the brain, which provides a unified perceptual field, binding the brain's disparate sensory, emotional, and thinking experiences together. Consciousness provides the screen so that you see the movie rather than the separate frames of film. It allows you to distinguish the undifferentiated mass of color that is forest, from the individual trees with their leaves and branches. It combines facial expressions, tone of voice, body language and words to formulate an impression of what someone else is communicating to you.

Consciousness is transcendent, making reality far deeper and richer by creating a wider context and broader perspective. The botanist sees a flower in one way, a poet another, a lover yet another. Two friends sit on a beach with the sand, salt air, sea breeze, sun, and sound of waves. One loves the beach and savors every moment, while the other is uncomfortable, preoccupied, and miserable. The vast panorama of human perceptual experience is thus very individual, and constantly changing during the course of a day.

Asking essential questions deepens your perspectives, and expands your consciousness.

Now Go Deeper
What specific essential question is vitally important for you to hold right now?

Your destiny is playing the music that you dance to, even if you can't yet hear it clearly. These letters are not a solution in search of a problem. Many young men are in crisis. The obstacles you face – both unique and universal challenges to conscious masculinity – are quite real: violence, painful isolation, relationship catastrophes, lack of meaningful work, or an early death from ignored health issues. Your natural, willful, mutinous, volcanic longing for a far away haven begins with the ambitious inquiry into your own wounds and suffering. I beg you to learn to embrace your own bamboozlement, to honor uncertainty as your teacher, to access the many resources available to you on the path to awakening. The world is the world in spite of all your wishes to the contrary. Most of all, I want you to understand that wherever you are right now is exactly where you need to be. There really is no better than here and now. You probably have been told this many times, but to make it your own, you must dwell within its truth as much as possible. There is no need to rush and no reason to procrastinate. *Mutatis mutandis*! The necessary changes having been made, you will gradually live more into your *own* life, as opposed to the one designed for you by your parents or society.

So much of your life energy is focused on the externals right now, with its intoxicating and confusing brew of relationships, work and engaging activities. Yet, your inner world is waiting, inviting you to explore limiting beliefs and unskillful habits, as well as inspiring perspectives and wellsprings of creativity. Such a voyage, like any other, requires some preparation in order to be successful. You need a curious mind, an open heart, and a willingness to face your demons. A map of the territory is also useful. These letters aspire to be that, a star chart of awareness, configurations of barrier reefs and emotional currents and tides, delineations of the contours of manhood. Welcome to the adventure! You are your own gift to the world, both who you are, and who you are becoming.

II

BEING A MAN

Always choose a conversation that empowers. There is a lot of negative noise about masculine bad in the world, and through conditioning you have incorporated this into what you constantly tell yourself about what it really means to be a man. One of the most essential aspects of growing into healthy manhood is to take total responsibility for everything you experience. This does not mean that you control or caused what happens: if your father beat or demeaned you as part of him releasing his own rage, that was not right, not fair and not your fault. You take responsibility by dealing with what that did to you inside, by not repeating that cycle and being destructive with your own anger. Do you see? This requires reflection, a willingness to examine some dark places, and a degree of emotional fluency.

Conditioning and advertising tell you not so much what to think, but what to think about. They fill you with chatter about maleness that is meaningless, and often do not validate your own journey. You have been exposed to hundreds of thousands of images and impressions up to this point in your life. Many created a faulty foundation of great lies upon which to build your notion of manhood. I have slowly come to understand that for an inner vital version of maleness to arise from this confusion requires that one carefully examine the falsehoods, and then choose to espouse a more inspired version. Consider these destructive, culturally powerful myths about masculinity:

A real man is a sturdy oak that feels no pain, has no fear, and needs no one. All the messages that have seeped into your being over many years of unconscious training have instilled in you some version of "might makes right," that fear and crying are signs of weakness, competition is king, and money and sexual prowess define your degree of maleness. You are seeking a diploma in masculinity that your family and the larger culture tells you can only be obtained through bashing your body through risky behaviors, sports, or the glorious playing field of battle. Open to the truth that fear, sadness and pain are your allies, not your enemies. They provide feedback that will only get louder if ignored.

Violence is the ultimate solution to solving problems. Violence is any mean word, look, sign, or act that hurts another person's body, feelings or things. The world needs less of it, not more versions of manhood that glorify it. This great lie suggests that the lines between good and evil are crystal clear, rather than the messy complexities that actually exist in human relations and conflicts. Collateral damage is often seen as just an unfortunate necessity, wholly justified by the outcome. The inconvenient truth of the cycle of violence – wherein an eye for an eye produces blindness in all, creating more problems than it solves – is simply ignored. Sometimes it takes more courage to walk away from a fight, and to engage your inner demons, rather than projecting them onto others. Every man must discover for himself where his instinct to protect both self and others crosses into mindless anger, or blind obedience to rules he does not believe have merit.

The great man theory. Your mind may be filled with ideas that only powerful individuals create important change, which unfortunately ignores the contributions of countless people, and the complex social circumstances that provided the fertile soil for the positive shifts to occur. Incredibly narrow and simplistic, history is filled mostly with the stories of great persons who were straight, white, male and able-bodied, largely ignoring women and people of color. This warped perspective also sustains the notion that "ordinary people" are powerless to effect change, unless they are saved by the force of some exceptional character. Outside of heroic fiction, such people are rare to nonexistent. The explorer fallacy is also destructive. The vast majority of famous trailblazers were actually traveling through places where tribal people already lived, getting both survival advice and local directions, rather than subduing untamed wilderness. How arrogant to say that somewhere was discovered only when your culture got there! And the natives were simply part of the terrain, a dehumanizing perspective that then justified claiming resources for oneself, over and over, as if the land were effectively uninhabited.

Adversity always strengthens you. This has been incessantly drummed into your emerging sense of what maleness is all about. Videogame and fictional characters often gain more and more skills, power, and accouterments as the story progresses. In short, they always become more capable, even as they experience both physical and psychological events that would crush the average person. Yet the on-screen champions always seem to just bounce back, despite levels of trauma that generally incapacitate. Combat soldiers who return with lifelong disabilities, older athletes past any possible peak performance, failed businesses, and other real life scenarios are simply discarded in the quest to super size a real man's prowess. Humans *do* overcome difficult challenges, but they don't do it magically and instantly on their own. They do so with a lot of support from others, and sufficient time to pull through, heal, and rally. And sometimes, they don't ever completely recover. **True heroes are always courageous, principled, skillful, selfless and inspiring**. This is quite a difficult mantle for the average man to embody. Inside, a hero is often full of doubt, and flawed by some trait that holds him back. With the help of a guide of some sort, heroes are able to transform—first themselves, and then the challenging situation. They get engaged by some inciting event, which propels them into action. So everyone is hero material. The ordinary world of your own self-doubt, and what you perceive as your deficits, is the starting point for your own personal hero's journey.

Being a man does involve walking the way of the warrior, just not the bang bang shoot- 'em-up Hollywood version. True heroes do exist, inspired beings who act with integrity in the pursuit of justice, and who have the capacity to channel the support of others into positive outcomes for the greater whole. Warrior energy involves discipline, which grows from within, and is about doing what you know is good and right for you. It is not a "have to," "ought to," or "should" imposed from outside. It ignores any considerations, distractions, or outside conditions that might arise: you're too tired, you'll do it tomorrow, or something else is demanding your time and energy. The origin of the word implies instruction, and discipline enlarges who you are, as well as your capacity to honor your commitments. It is an inner fire that surges through the inevitable resistance that arises. It is suspending the war within of conflicting desires, in order to do what needs to be done. Discipline teaches you to embrace everything, especially that which is difficult. It accepts that the long plateaus, when nothing really seems to be moving forward, are fertile ground, where trust and self-confidence are built. Those moments are accomplishing something in you that cannot yet be recognized, a slow forging of the *athame*, or healing dagger, whose purpose is to ritually cut away that which no longer serves you.

Now Go Deeper
What are the three most important qualities of conscious masculinity you wish to embody?

The warrior is boldly visible to himself—both strengths and weaknesses. He does not hide from unpleasant truths, but strives to live with integrity—meaning he tells the truth, keeps agreements, honors his commitments, and respects and values the contributions of others. He is ever vigilant and ruthless in cutting through his own negative *mindtalk* and self-defeating behaviors. This involves a constant letting go of anything that does not serve his growth. He understands that clear, persistent, and calm effort over time in small tasks creates great internal changes. Discipline and integrity are the tools that forge your authenticity, so that your deepest inner values exist in harmony with your external mode of living. It is possible to become comfortable in your maleness, despite the prevalent destructive distortions about manhood, and poor modeling by so many of the human species. There is no shortage of random, destructive, inaccurate information about what it means to be a man. It is up to you to sift through your own conditioning, to discover for yourself what rings true. As you live what seems right to you, you will deepen your understanding of the masculine psyche. You will learn to embrace your power, and realize that most obstacles ultimately issue from within. Keep peace in your heart, yet do not neglect to hone the skills required to defend and protect. The warrior's finest qualities enable you to create a new internal conversation about being male—one that empowers you to be the best man you can, right here and now.

III

THE NATURE OF THE JOURNEY

Energy follows attention and awareness creates choice. These simple principles, once ingrained, greatly enhance your ability to forge a path through this lifetime. They are the foundation of using your intentionality to create the kind of life you want. You are a sentient entity, a sensing-feeling-thinking being on this beautiful planet, and that is an enormous privilege and adventure in itself. From squirrels and birds building nests in a city park, to wolves hunting in packs, to elk moving down in the fall from the high country of a wilderness forest, nature everywhere embodies two basic pulses: survive and evolve. This is true even if you live in highly urban environs. You are a part of nature, an animal with much more in common with other creatures of the earth, than not.

Imagine the profound developmental steps that have brought you to reading and holding this book in your hand. Appreciate the complexity and interconnectedness of that process. Do you see how your individual physical growth mimics the evolution of the human species, and the expansion of your awareness invokes the origins of consciousness? What have you been doing up until this point in your life? Surviving and evolving! What will you do for the rest of your life? Survive and evolve. How that reality unfolds for you is a bittersweet mixture of nature and nurture. Choice sets the stage for empowering mindsets and beneficial actions, thus increasing confidence and skills — an uplifting whirl of enrichment.

All the vitality to create and forge your personal odyssey begins with the principle that energy follows attention. Where is your attention right now? Likely dancing back and forth between an external focus – reading this book – and internally directed thinking about its content and how it applies to your life. With unrelated random thoughts, feelings, and sensations also occurring. Play with the focus and flow of your attention, the footprint of consciousness in the body. Put your awareness fully on your index finger. Now point it at the sky and shift your attention there. Now move it to the spaciousness inside your ribcage. Being completely present to what is happening here and now is not an easy undertaking in our multitasking, constant stim, info overloaded world. Yet the more you develop the habit of directing your attention – both inside and outside dimensions – the more you will unlock unbelievable stores of energy. You have undoubtedly experienced many moments of flow in your life, when things seem easy, effortless, light and playful. More gets done when you're having fun! Playing team sports, engaging in hiking, biking, skiing or riding horses, music, dancing, and sex are all good examples where flow can more easily arise. Mind body and emotions are all aligned as each moment unfolds. Cultivating flow in all aspects of your daily existence is dependent on keeping your attention immersed in the here and now.

Life is about learning lessons, some of which you may think stupid or irrelevant. Every day you are given teachings, and how you respond to them affects both your inner sense of peace and contentment, and what you are able to manifest in the outer world. These consciousness exercises are repeated until learned. There are no mistakes, only lessons— and the learning never ends. Please do not compare your school classroom experiences with the laboratory of existence. The lifelong discovery required to have a good life is self-directed and often non-linear. And whenever one door closes, another will surely open, sometimes in very unanticipated ways. You have the capacity to reflect upon and contemplate what is happening to you. My own life path suggests that if you want your potential to flower into the fullness of your manhood, you must pay attention to what is happening *inside* you, as well as the external forces of the outside world. Think about any form of sports or even a video game: do you want to play it intelligently and improve by learning more and more with each round, or are you content to be destroyed in the same spot every time, by the identical monster over and over? Your mind and life are shaped by how you use them.

Be a good animal first by exploring your own body, a marvel of engineering, form and function. Learn what you can do with it. Tap into its rhythms to understand how you function best. Investigate how to relax and release – in healthy ways – the inevitable stresses of everyday modern existence. Your body is the temple within which you find yourself, and every life experience you have is rooted within it. You need not become a full time fakir, monk or yogi to learn to care for and respect it, even as you sometimes test its limits. It is challenging for any man to completely accept and love his body. Most often there are various flaws in either functioning or appearance that he prefers would be different. Women are clearly adversely affected by the insidious "not measuring up" that advertising aggressively portrays. Men, unfortunately, are also subtly trained to believe that everything from a large penis to perfect six-pack abs, and a full head of hair, are requisites for a happy life.

Look around in your immediate environs, and celebrate the plethora of body types and physical characteristics. The diversity is mind-boggling. For you to survive in the best possible shape for as long as possible, you must learn to care for your corpus, tend to its needs. To do that it helps to appreciate your body, which means you must accept or work to change what you can. When the inevitable breakdowns occur, listen to the feedback it offers you, which will always guide you towards healing. It is a powerfully true cliché that without optimum health, everything becomes more challenging. There is a fiesta of possibility for maximizing functionality, whatever limitations you might have, as Stephen Hawking – and other less famous yet equally determined folks – clearly demonstrate every day.

Bodies need to be in motion, get wholesome nutrition, and adequate, regular rest. Absolutely learn the basics of healthy cooking and eating – perhaps even grow some of your own food – a very satisfying and enlivening endeavor. Find some regular way to move your body in ways you enjoy that foster the fitness triad of strength, suppleness and stamina. Take a basic Cardio-Pulmonary-Resuscitation and first aid course. When you are paying attention and "in touch" on these very fundamental levels, then this awareness creates choice. Stay out late with your friends, or get more rest because something important is happening tomorrow? Eat that junk food now, or wait to put something more nutritious into your body? It's very easy to go on autopilot and mindlessly pick options that ultimately do not serve you. Life always provides consequences and feedback related to your actions. Developing robust self-care habits is challenging when you first start, but they have an undeniable impact on your day-to-day as well as your future.

Now Go Deeper
Make a quick list of your salubrious routines. Anything important missing in how you regularly nurture yourself?

Many men have grown up learning a great lie: that your mind and body are separate entities. Everything is connected. Your thoughts influence your feelings, and both impact your body. Your mind is like a wild horse that you must learn to ride. Wondrous imagination, creativity and important insights issue forth from it, as do obsessing, worrying, future tripping, and addictive impulses. Focus the lens of self-observation on your mind—just as important as the awareness you are learning to hold around your body. Optimal mental health includes emotional, psychological and social wellbeing. It allows you to cope with life stressors, realize your own potential, and contribute to the whole. Don't believe everything you think is supremely sage advice. Every mind abhors a void, so it fills it with fantastical stories and calls them truth!

Stimulating your brain, challenging it, avoiding the equivalent of junk food in terms of what you expose it to regularly, will enhance your mindset and create a positive spiral of development. Learn to enjoy the stillness of the deep woods, the starry sky time, the gift of an amazing museum, the wildness of rivers and oceans, the splendor of a live music concert. This incredible planet, of which you are a part, welcomes you. Embrace the everyday gifts that nature freely bestows upon you. Use absolutely everything in service to awakening. Awareness is not an intellectual exercise. It is a participatory reprogramming that supports your development in every situation, and has a significant effect upon your ability to remain centered and connected amidst life's inevitable challenges. It is the antidote to living an unexamined life of conditioned responses. Life is ceaselessly inviting you to willingly step into the unknown, to get lost within the world, and thereby enlarge who you really are.

IV

PARENTS

Parents are often wrong. They either do too much or too little, never just enough. Yet they are always doing the best they can, given their own upbringing and challenges. At this point in our species development, humans don't yet know how to consistently support babies and children into becoming healthy, happy, loving, intelligent, creative adults. Every child receives both gifts and wounds from their parents, and your job is to learn to appreciate the gifts, even as you attempt to mend the emotional injuries. We all want to be put together right, and fix things as an adult that hurt us as a child. The subconscious marches to its own beat, ever towards healing. You cannot change the past, but you can alter your relationship to it. Be willing to explore the darkness of some of the difficulties you experienced, and slowly connect the dots to see how those early episodes still influence you.

Everyone harbors a Shadow, a repository of repressed emotions they would prefer to conceal. It takes both courage and support to look at parts of yourself that were rejected by your parents, society, and even you. All those times when you felt misunderstood, the "you're too..."put downs, or the "you're not enough" shaming, those little wounds that happen in families, and the big traumas that occur as well. If you can name it you can tame it. Your Shadow is a natural part of the self, a reservoir of human darkness, the storehouse of your lifelong core issue—and also the wellspring of creative expression. Exploring and embracing it helps you avoid doing to others what was done to you, thereby breaking the destructive cycle. Growing up with violence, substance abuse, or mental illness in your original family of origin generated significantly negative impacts on your life trajectory. You unconsciously called upon the extraordinary impulse to survive. Maybe that involved using substances to hide your own pain, acting out aggressively to release your frustration, or withdrawing into loneliness and isolation, living inside the agony of not fitting in. Honor whatever you did in the past to survive the wounds from your parents.

My own life experience tells me that it is possible to move beyond whatever pain you've been living, and not stay trapped in that drama. As you drop down the rabbit hole of dysfunctional family dynamics, and begin to sift through your personal deck of memory cards, it can feel like a snowstorm viewed through the windshield of a slow moving vehicle—jagged refractions with heartbreaking intensity. Often there are just loose memory threads, unraveling disturbing feelings and images transferred from one generation to another, swirling bits of deeply troubling, gruesome narratives you would prefer to keep hidden. This Shadow creates patterns of reaction with unseen cause; it is present and absent at the same time, and comprises the emotional baggage you drag around in your interior spaces. It contributes to your own poor choices, bad behavior and abusive tendencies. Whenever you become upset by the remarks or actions of another, this buried material is activated, causing you to respond unskillfully. What whispers in the dark hasn't found its voice yet.

One of the most important injuries you must acknowledge and address is the Father Failure, a messy confusing morass of hurt, disappointment, fear and anger. Every man has one. Yuck! Who wants to go there? My dad and I got along just fine until I actually developed a personality of my own! You may find yourself striving to become the man you wished your father had been. Or perhaps you are endlessly engaged in pleasing him, trying to get his approval, even as you rebel against what he seems to stand for. For many young men, the Father Failure is largely about growing up without a consistently present father or other positive male figure taking an interest in them and their lives. This father hunger often produces acting out aggressive behaviors—really a cry for help, in an attempt to get the attention they crave. For others it is that persistent nagging feeling that whatever they do and accomplish, they never quite measure up.

The Mommy Mangle is usually subtler. But it is there as well, often in forms of being babied, manipulated emotionally, or clung to. While maternal instincts to serve and protect can be incredibly strong, they may feel different to the male child, who experiences being smothered or ignored. Mothers especially are challenged during the teen years, when they may not understand why you retreat to your cave and just want to be left alone. Their attempts to help may feel invasive. Especially if they have courageously survived as a single parent, they may inadvertently use you for emotional support, or as a crutch that explains why – with some hidden resentment – they did not focus more on other aspects of their lives. Perhaps they brought home men who were unkind to you in various ways.

When confronting the confusion of these heartaches, the purpose is not to harshly judge parents, but rather to specifically name the wounds that need healing. Sibling relationships are also a part of it. Did you support or torment each other as you each experienced different versions of your parents? Do you ever talk about any of it? Do unspoken, hurtful offenses between you keep you apart, rather than close?

Your early family experiences are the threads out

of which you weave your story. Making peace with your parents is one of the most important steps you can take on the road to fully empowered adulthood. It is rarely an easy or pleasant path, but a vital one to embrace, and more liberating than an ongoing festival of recrimination. Explore anything that was hidden, opening yourself to feel everything within your Shadow. All those unfulfilled promises and maladaptive connections – years in the making – take time to unwind and unravel. Then forgiveness may find a foothold, framing your past with greater equanimity. Finally, the space opens for celebrating the gifts, the good things that were also transmitted to you during childhood. These presents are sometimes hidden within the darkness, and can only be accessed by first cracking open the shell of understanding. You can't appreciate the parents you have until you grieve the loss of the parents you wanted.

There are many different ways to access buried childhood hurt: talking with siblings, other relatives or friends, journaling, therapy, co-counseling. The guiding principle is that you are as sick as you are secret—for a wound to heal it must be exposed to air and light. The highly charged dramas and negative traumas that occur in families are often undisclosed to the outside world. Starting with the rottenest memory apple may be too difficult, but you can begin by recalling smaller attacks on your childhood innocence. The goal here is not the endless repetition of the story, which only keeps you stuck in it, but rather clearly revealing and speaking the truth of what was. Then all the trapped feelings – which have been buried alive along with the painful memory – are allowed to find free expression. This gradual dismantling of the Shadow occurs over years, not days or weeks. It is the only way to free yourself from patterns that otherwise will continue to run you.

Now Go Deeper
Start with a simple list. Think of one parent, and then write at the top of the page "I resent..." Allow the stuck hurts and irritations to flow on the paper.

It is not about sending this Fed Ex to your parent once you are done. Celebrate! You don't have to live out the unrealized dreams of your parents, to meet whatever expectations they have imposed on *your* life. For better and worse, you are standing on the shoulders of your ancestors, those who came before. Learn to pay homage, appreciate and give thanks to them, for they gave you life itself, roots and wings. The roots of your culture – including language, food and customs – ground and enliven your life. The wings of self-confidence and support enable you to fashion the kind of life you want for yourself. In my home, I have a bookshelf that contains photos and some memorabilia dedicated to my ancestors. It reminds me that my way is easier because of their efforts. It also honors that I have overcome some of the wounds I received from them, that forgiveness has blossomed with time and attention. Praise your naked brokenness, if only in private. Immerse your childhood wounds in the color of the ocean after a long sensuous sunset. Embrace the light of self-awareness among the ruins of your terrible childhood, and discover the guidance to be found in the rubble. Shape the struggles of your early years into something of meaning and beauty. Strive to abolish the delusions and ignorant prejudices of those who came before, and to pass on to the next generation a little less confusion about how to be in the world. Remember that you are not held back by the love you didn't get in the past, but by the love you're not giving in the present.

V

DEMYSTIFYING EMOTIONS

All feelings are okay. All behaviors are not! Becoming emotionally fluent is one of the most important skills to embrace. This means learning how to be in touch with what you are feeling inside, so that you can communicate these sensations to yourself and others, in ways that are life enhancing rather than destructive. The direct immediate fleeting sensations of feelings are like a navigational compass, pointing to the basic directions: mad, sad, glad, afraid, or disgusted. These basic feelings might be conceptualized as the primary colors of emotional states. Often the time between what is triggering a feeling, and the feeling itself, can be instantaneous. This is very useful for survival. Bypassing the analytic mind, feelings quickly mobilize you into action with adaptability and speed. You are on alert, with a flashing discernment about whether someone is a danger or to be trusted, a situation is safe or threatening. Sacrificing accuracy for swiftness, feelings just arise in rapid

41

response to external stimuli, or more slowly to the flow of internal thoughts.

Emotions, on the other hand, are complicated states that involve a whole portrait of thoughts, feelings and body sensations. They take the basic palette of primary feelings and paint profound and complex experiences, such as shame, grief or honor. Emotions have been described as energy in motion: Fear is the energy to do your best in a new situation, guilt is the energy for personal change, unworthiness keeps you on track, hurt feelings remind you how much you care, anger is the fuel for creating boundaries and change, discouragement reveals your courage. Think of feelings and emotions as internal weather, often changing throughout the day. Even as they leave an echo that vibrates through your whole being, their chaotic primitive nature is what enlivens your experience, brings you out of your head and into the body. Moods occur when a dominant emotion persists, often creating a more turbulent fluctuation in the quality of your internal barometer. Moods last longer but are also ever shifting, so be grateful for high moods and graceful during the low ones.

Most likely, the people who taught you the essentials of dealing with your emotional life were totally confused! What was modeled was probably a troubling mix of repression, mindless expression of anger, a consuming tempest of anxiety, or varying and pervasive layers of unresolved sadness. They unconsciously appropriated this multigenerational mélange of misconceptions and then passed them on to you. You have no doubt adopted some of the same patterns as your own, even though they do not serve you. In addition, men also get a heavy dose of cultural conditioning, telling them that real men don't cry, don't express their pain, and don't experience fear. From frat boys to business dudes, many males are trapped in a paradigm that squashes and represses fear and sorrow. The allowable masculine emotional keyboard is thus limited to anger and occasional raucous happiness. Hardly a prescription for a full and rich life! Exercising your emotional muscles has great rewards, even if your first workouts are in private. Emotional fluency enables you to "just be" with whatever feeling, emotion or mood is arising, rather than deny, fight or control it. The energy is still primitive, raw and wild, but skillfully domesticated. With time and attention, you'll recognize the physical feedback your body is giving you when a particular feeling state is present.

Repeatedly reacting strongly with anger, fear or sadness to a given stimulus is always an indication that some past hurt wants to be healed. When you find yourself being triggered by a remark, gesture, facial expression or other action from someone else, just pause. The simple act of stopping allows you to create a longer fuse, to step back and take a larger perspective, to remove yourself from any stance of victimhood, and to reduce drama. When someone is dumping their garbage, the pause allows you to not overreact, to step back from the trash they are spewing about and not let it fall on you. By not piling pain on top of pain with those close to you, you can remember the love, and maybe find some humor, even in difficult circumstances.

You can stay relaxed and open in the face of a fear attack, stress, or any disruptive emotional state by centering. Centering allows you to blend and flow with the current situation, rather than block and resist it, by grounding you in the present moment and rebalancing your emotions. It is the essence of how to actually "let it flow and let it go." Practice it first on your own. This helps build the capacity to use it during difficult interactions with others. To center, simply bring your attention inside to consciously and positively affect your sensory systems: breathe deeply, close your eyes, visualize, and utter a mantric sound, if you are comfortable with that. Rather than reacting habitually, pause and begin with the breath. Slowly breathe in through your nose and hold the breath, each for a count of four. Then breathe out through pursed lips, relaxing your facial muscles, for a count of eight. With each breath, you can intentionally allow your abdominal breathing to get slower, quieter and more regular. Breathing in, you are present to whatever is, Breathing out, you calm yourself, and shift to a more empowered state.

Your breath is the bridge from where you are to where you'd like to be. Ride the waves of your breath to a calmer, safer place. When you use the breath to center yourself in the present moment, you apply minimum effort to achieve maximum results. It generates stability and energy. You order your physiology, balance your emotions, and harmonize your thoughtstream to optimize flow. Greater access to intuition and clear, problem-solving thinking arises. Such awareness will create choice about how you then respond to emotionally difficult situations, and help you to understand what *you* need in that moment. Defense or counter-attack is not your only option. Centering lets your system know you are safe, by activating your right brain and parasympathetic nervous system. This has the effect of suspending the cognitive mind's negative thoughts and the limbic system's feelings, which allows the body to fully relax. This is how you will gradually shift the blind stimulus-reaction patterns. A centered person lives out of possibility rather than expectation.

Another useful practice is the reframe, wherein you transform the spiral of negative emotions by using creative playfulness, an adult version of the childhood game, "let's pretend..." This is not pushing away the feelings, but shifting their intensity so they do not escalate into destructive behaviors. Whenever you notice a difficult state arising, you can pause and fashion a different perspective. The crying baby on an airplane becomes a healing vessel discharging all the negative energy on the planet; the barking dogs keeping you from sleep are really talking about you in very complimentary ways; the jitters before giving a public speech become electric excitement surrounding you with positive glowing energy; your sadness about a friend's illness transforms into flowers falling around his smiling face. Using your unbounded imagination, you can invent a different perception of reality, moment to moment, whenever annoyance, anxiety, or despondency threaten to overwhelm you. More than providing just momentary distractions, this simple reframing technique transforms a turbulent emotional situation into a more empowering one.

Now Go Deeper
Make a list of some of the small, external stimuli that bothered you in the past couple of days. Pick one, and briefly write about how you reacted. Now, reframe it.

You may be considered an adult chronologically, but that in no way guarantees that *emotionally* you are one. Many men go through their lives and never develop any practical understanding of how their own emotions run them. Regular check-ins can help you enlarge your own vocabulary for your different feelings and emotional states. A monthly practice of journaling about whatever is in your heart can be of great assistance in observing the persistent patterns that need changing, and for focusing on new modalities of expression. *How am I feeling right now?* is an empowering simple query that expands feeling sensitivity. Finally, regularly examine what were the best and worst parts of an experience, your day or weekend. Each of these three practices will incrementally expand your capacity to be emotionally fluent. There are times when you may just want to fully experience a given emotion, to surrender to its intensity; in other moments, centering or reframing can be of assistance to modify the intensity of the situation. The key here is choice. Having some different tools available creates more possibility. Being emotionally armored, constantly compartmentalizing, repressing, or destructively discharging feelings, takes a significant toll on your body over the years. The energy locked in such stale mindsets and old stories of who you are can be released and channeled. You jettison from your backpack of habits whatever no longer serves, lightening your load and your whole being. It is not an easy or straightforward path, but one that will lead you to a better life.

VI

ANGER

It is particularly useful for men to take on the role of detective when approaching their anger. Men have been conditioned to accept the male emotional funnel, where many different feelings are channeled into anger because it is viewed as their "acceptable" primary feeling. Anger is not good or bad, it just is. It lives in your body, fueled by the protective fight-or-flight reaction, a powerful brew of biochemical messengers designed to help you survive. Pupils dilate, pulse increases, blood flows to extremities, breathing increases in depth and frequency, blood sugar and adrenal hormones increase. Where exactly does it begin in you – neck, back, stomach, elsewhere – those first indications that you are getting irritated? As you explore the continuum of this feeling, the idea is to tune into the feedback from your body while you are still at a lower intensity on the dial—mildly annoyed or peeved. Because anger lives in your body, it is very dependent on how the environment is adversely affecting your physiology. Whenever you are hot, cold, hungry or tired, your irritability will be affected. Does your anger meter consistently jump from zero to one hundred with the slightest provocation, from serene to screaming in the blink of a moment? Notice where you first begin to sense its tension, and with time you can shift your response by using a coping strategy earlier in the reaction. In effect, you begin to reset your habitual anger meter to a lower setting.

What triggers repeatedly stimulate you getting mad? What is alive within you, that habitually responds with anger? Be curious about it, rather than denying it. When compared with what many humans experience each day in trying to survive, many of your daily irritations pale in significance. Your own expectations and sense of entitlement are often what fuel you repeatedly being triggered in similar situations—bad weather, traffic jam, long supermarket line, car, home or electronic breakdowns, bureaucracy or business clerk unhelpful with a DGAS attitude. It is not about whether the expectations are reasonable or not. Just realize they contribute to anger arising when not fulfilled.

Whenever you find yourself embroiled in anger over and over in similar circumstances, look for the layer of fear or sadness that underlies it. Again, because of developmental training, your default setting often reverts to expressing anger, even when something else is really being played on your emotional keyboard. An example might be reacting when your child carelessly runs into the street, or a teen breaks curfew without calling, or a friend does not show up for an important meet. The initial response of anger may actually be covering a fear that they might get or be hurt. Men who experience a great loss sometimes react with anger and irritability, because accessing the sad or scared feelings seems too vulnerable and unfamiliar.

Often it is not immediately clear what you are feeling. You just are upset, and anger may simply be the habitual response. These emotional patterns run deep. Some men are unable to access their anger— a reaction to growing up around males who were always angry, so they decided they would never be like that. Early family dynamics greatly influence habitual modes of expressing and responding to anger. Take the contemplative time to uncover the roots of your destructive patterns. Remember that resentments are simply trapped anger—negative feelings you continue to carry, rather than release and let go of. Holding onto them is drinking poison and expecting the other person to die. Regularly flush resentments by journaling, or skillfully working out the conflict with the involved person.

How to cope with angry energy? You might talk it out, take a time out, exercise it out, dance it out, write it out, art it out, but it needs to be released in ways that are not destructive to yourself or others. Again, some inner explorations will help find what works best for you. Focusing on cultivating patience can cause much daily anger to wither at the mild irritation stage. The power of waiting can transform the tyranny of urgency, by directing your mental thoughtstream train into the station of appreciation for what is happening right here and now. Presence is the essence of patience, supported by compassion and loving kindness toward the situation, a willingness to stay with *what is*, rather than demanding *what you want it to be*.

Finally, how does one respond skillfully to someone else's angry energy? People you find difficult are great teachers. Be thankful for their presence in your life! Realize that when someone is pointing a finger at you, they are just trying to discharge their own pain and discomfort. They're just not doing it skillfully, because they are caught up in their own conditioned reactions to being angry. What to do when their negative, blaming, shaming, angry energy is directed at you? À la Star Trek, "Shields up and Open a Channel!" In other words, protect yourself and try to understand what their need really is. When they are emotionally dumping their garbage, you need to give space, both emotionally and physically, and not have it land on you.

The angrier that two people are at each other, the more distance they need to have separating them, for safety reasons. Don't get hooked! Two people out of control with their emotions definitely can't successfully problem solve. Often, the angry person will try to trigger you, in an attempt to have you join them in their temporary dance of insanity. The "open a channel" skillful action is to stay connected. By this I do not mean becoming similarly emotionally engaged, but rather communicating that you recognize they are upset, and you want to clearly understand what they would like to be different. People often use anger as an unskillful way to create boundary or establish connection. *Connect first, then redirect.* This is a basic martial arts principle, especially utilized in Aikido, which recognizes that you cannot change the aggressive energy coming toward you without first accepting it. You remain present, open and centered – something that requires practice and discipline – in the face of someone yelling or threatening you.

This can be scary at first, but you can do it safely by maintaining distance – out of striking reach – and standing slightly to the side of their non-dominant hand. You first acknowledge and empathize with their upset, and only then suggest calmly that they either take a time out, or in some way rebalance themselves. You further shift the situation by inquiring what might be helpful for them right now. When you focus on their underlying need, you direct their energy towards a solution, rather than just conditioned mindless release. The course of a conflict is determined not by the initiator, but by how one responds to the opening salvo. I struggled with my own anger for many years, until I gradually understood and embodied what I am sharing with you in this letter.

Now Go Deeper
Think about the last two times you were angry. How did you react and express it?

Would you say that you usually engage positively with this emotion, releasing it without harm to others or self, so that its hold over you gradually diminishes? Or are you still stuck in mindless explosive rage, where any amount of subsequent penitence fails to undo the damage caused by the outburst? Are you trapped in repressed or numbing patterns, that only cause the unexpressed, unresolved anger of resentments to contaminate your interactions in unproductive ways? Do you sometimes use anger as a way to feel alive? Only through being curious when anger arises anywhere on its continuum—from mild annoyance to outright rage—can you become more skillful in dealing with this powerful emotion. This serves you much better than denying or harshly judging your behaviors. Many men stay stuck in their anger patterns – an ungainly beast lying dormant within because they do not reflect upon or contemplate how they wield this energy in the world.

Anger, aggression and violence are related but distinct constructs. It is possible to be angry without expressing it aggressively or with violence, but for some individuals they are all wired up together. It is not healthy for yourself, or those around you, to be subjected to your emotional explosions. So, if this is an issue for you, stop pretending that you are okay and learn some skills. Find some peaceful role models—men who are infrequently provoked to anger, who have learned to manage their stress and pressure in positive ways. Find new ways to ask for what you would like, or to speak your truth without an angry edge to your voice, words or actions. Experiment with how to release the beast through exercise, meditation, humor, journaling, better communication, or creative outlets.

VII

FEAR

Fear is a one-note song whose only lyric is stop. It is such a common and popular tune because the stark reality is that anything can happen at any time. Even that clever repository of daily wisdom – the bumper sticker – proclaims, "Shit happens," as well as the antidote, "Shift happens." At any moment the cosmic flyswatter may strike, the great goof will deliver something unpleasant, and circumstances will only get worse. The more you flinch beneath the shadow of the unknown, the more constricted your life becomes. Fear is not something you will easily overcome, but you need to do your best to understand how it functions, and how to work with its reality in your life.

Fear is a useful survival mechanism that has enabled humans to endure, both individually and as a species. In terms of physical threat, it allows you to react quickly, bypassing the more plodding cognitive brain functions. No time to contemplate the tree that is falling on you, or your hand on the hot pan, or the fist heading for your face. You react first, physiologically and with your whole being, to get out of harm's way. Fight, flight, and even freeze, are biologically programmed responses meant to be allies, signals to be heeded. The physiology of fear is based on the fight or flight reaction, and is actually very similar to the sensation of excitement. Like anger, fear is not good or bad, it simply *is*. It is pointless to deny its presence when it arises. You cannot alter its cautionary, constrictive energy until you first accept it.

Fear has many disguises, and everyone has a default favorite that grips and holds them back:

You are not good enough. This common form of conditioning bathes many in fear from an early age—a deeply ingrained sense that something is wrong with you, that you are irreparably, fatally flawed. Shame is, at its core, fear of disconnection because you are somehow not worthy. Fears of being rejected, condemned, abandoned or alone, generate worries about being defective or inadequate, unworthy of being loved or wanted—thus fueling a circular cycle of deeper apprehension. This basic fear can also manifest as incessantly comparing yourself to others—an energy draining habit that only keeps you blocked. It indicates that your self-esteem – your overall evaluation of your own worth – is on shaky ground, and needs to be enhanced by healing some old inner wounds.

Fear of missing out (FOMO). The concern is that you will not get your needs met. This sense of deprivation, of not having an experience or getting something, makes you anxious. Only control assures you something essential will not be withheld. Tightening your grasp on power, money, position or health ultimately leads to a chronic dissatisfaction that erodes your sense of wellbeing. Impatience is a cousin of fear. The more you hurry, the more likely you are to stumble. You'll begin to see that rushing, impatience, and control are really forms of violence against yourself and others.

Loss of self. Death is the ultimate mediator of this one. The fear of death is actually, in part, a fear of not living life to its fullest. You may fear loss of the self with another person, by being dominated or overwhelmed emotionally. Fear – disguised as loss of self – frequently arises following physical, emotional or mental injury.

You will not be able to handle loss. Many fears involve the threat of loss: of control, love, acceptance, reputation, health, material goods, or life itself. The sense that you will not deal well with loss keeps you in place, holds you back, and prevents you from exploring your edge. Illness, losing a loved one, being fired, whatever might happen—you are scared you will not find the inner or outer resources to deal with it. So it is best to always play it safe as much as possible.

Now Go Deeper
Give two of your most dominant fears nicknames.
Get more friendly and familiar with them. Call them
by name whenever they show up.

Chronic anxiety is simply stuck fear. Unnamed,
unacknowledged and unmet, it magnifies the possibility of impending doom, becomes a pool of undifferentiated, unexpressed feelings that have amassed
over the years: sentiments you did not want to face,
impulses you were unwilling to honor. This mael-
strom produces a sense of chronic disempowerment,
dissipating your precious life energy into a past that
no longer exists or a future that has not yet come.
Chronic anxiety and its attendant pattern of worrying
keeps you locked in an unmediated tension between
the future, "can I?" and the past, "I should or ought to
have." This vicious, constricting whirlpool squeezes
out the present moment, which is where your power
lies. It can drown out what life is communicating to
you. Fear is always an emotional fast forward to an
imagined, negative future you want desperately to re-
strain. Where there is fear, there is often no listening.
What fear has to teach you can be lost if you keep
analyzing it, which only keeps you stuck; *thinking*
about it, or attempting to dominate it, turns you away
from it, but *awareness* turns you toward it.

How would you be with a frightened child? Accept fear, investigate it, hold the fear in your arms
with utmost care, caress it with understanding and

compassion, and then act in the face of it. Just note it is there and accept it. When a powerful wind blows the leaf trembles, yet you do not call it a coward; be a leaf in the wind when fear grips you. And sometimes you will want to cry and run and collapse crumpled in a corner, shudder in the darkness. Even though men are very good at hiding it, the truth is that everyone experiences being afraid, and at times is paralyzed by it. Observe your mind's private darkroom of negative thoughts, which will develop into fears if allowed free rein.

The same energy of fear that wants to constrict also provides the possibility to leap. The major theme song here is to let go of trying to control anything, and instead embrace fear's rough edges and mysterious qualities. You can't always figure your way out of life's problems, you need to just flow with them and let them go. The lessons in powerlessness will continue until you experience fear's naked truth. You can, however, consciously dial back your uneasiness. As you declare your fears, and develop skills to move through them, their power over you, and the desire to escape, will dissipate. Fear is always a guest in the living room of your emotions, and you have the power to ask it to quiet down or leave. But first and foremost you must acknowledge its presence!

Moving beyond your comfort zone always involves fear, discomfort and – ultimately – growth. From the first day of kindergarten, "feel the fear and do it anyway" needs to be inculcated into the hearts of young people, via refrigerator magnets and cereal box advertising. Part of this exploration is really being willing to notice how much of your life is constructed around stability and security, as opposed to nurturing your spirit, and hearing the call of the wild within. In many ways, your fears create the contrast that allows you to appreciate and value that which you love. Its shadows create depth and add meaning to your life. Fear's vibrations contrast with the great yes of love, that vast and endless canvas upon which you paint the picture of your life.

Looking at what you are most afraid of, you will find behind it what you most cherish. For every fear you encounter, there is something you love hidden in its cloak. Within the fear of losing your health lies the love of being able to have the energy and well-being to enjoy moving your body. Behind the fear of losing your family or friends rests the deep love of being connected, both giving and receiving appreciation. From the sharp, bracing apprehension of an adventure, to the butterfly qualms before an important event, to intellectual, abstract concerns about the state of the planet, fear is there to generate motion. It becomes a problem when you are paralyzed and limited by its grip. Healthy fear actually triggers instinct and intuition. With repeated training, you can stay relaxed and open in the face of a fear attack or extreme stress. Rather than become too stupid with panic to use your native creative intelligence, centering is a gentle way of stopping any reactive patterns by treating yourself with kindness, and affirming your ability to respond, to stand strong in the stillness of the raging river. It encourages you to create a personal spell for bolstering your own failing courage, in the face of whatever fear may be present. Over time you can become more skillful at recognizing when fear is present, accepting and shifting it in the moment by centering, and then making choices and taking wholehearted action from a more grounded place.

VIII

SADNESS

Life consistently offers up lessons in powerlessness, often in the intense form of personal illness or injury, death of a loved one, dissolution of a treasured relationship, or some other disturbing loss. Sadness is anytime, sadness is everywhere, involves anyone. A misery fest lurks behind the scenes in the happiest of moments, sneaks up around the corner to surprise you, wraps around you like a heavy garment you cannot shake off. Sadness delivers low energy, emotional pain and grief—a uniquely personal manifestation of a universal experience. Within its wildly unanticipated dimensions, its memories can claw inside you like a trapped animal, and its numbness can tint every event with darkened hues. Human sadness and hurt is like lightning; it does not choose its targets but strikes with no regard for position, success or moral stature. Everyone hears the grave and tender notes of tragedy at some point. Everything becomes colored by your anguish, and even hope seems a form of delusion.

Please learn to distinguish bourgeois hardship and inconvenience from true misery and universal agony. Something you wanted to buy, a broken favorite object, a flight delayed, or a flat tire—versus a child dying in your arms from famine, or a loved one seriously injured in a tornado. If you can fix it with a checkbook – yours or someone else's – then it probably does not really qualify as a " painful problem." Each of these might make you miserable and generate sadness, but get real with yourself and take the larger view. Being human, pain is inevitable but suffering is largely optional. You produce suffering when you create unnecessary additional distress by attempting to control or defend against the natural tumultuous experiences that all humanity shares—aging, illness, and loss of loved ones. Suffering arises when you do not accept what is, and the pain that goes with it. Suffering always involves not wanting what is, whether it be certain external circumstances, or inner thoughts, emotions, or physical sensations.

The first impulse may be to push sadness away, denying, minimizing or otherwise avoiding feeling it, with accompanying spastic efforts to put a smiley face on things. Sitting still leaves spaces for grief to get in. Part of the incessant busyness that many people demonstrate is just another foil preventing them from actually feeling their sadness. Getting lost in their heads, with guilt and regret warring with each other for dominance, is another avoidance tactic. For now, understand that both regret and guilt can be big rocks you carry around in your emotional backpack. Both grieving and self-forgiveness ask you in different ways to lighten that load. Just as worry can feed a chronic form of fear, unprocessed guilt and regret often fuel an ongoing, deep-seated sense of sadness, building blocks for a pyramid of pain that becomes increasingly difficult to scale.

Depression is a general, pervasive sadness. You may have a brain biochemistry that predisposes you to extended periods of melancholy, with attendant low energy, down mood, challenging shifts in sleep, eating and sexual function, and loss of pleasure from things you normally enjoy. Most depressed people who attempt suicide do not want to die, they just want the pain and sadness to stop, and see no other way out. Medication can help, and is essential in some cases to ease the burdens, so the inner transformative work can begin in earnest. However, there are no skills with just pills. Anti-depressants should *never* be suddenly stopped, because of an increased risk of suicide. Combating depression involves being willing to go down into your sadness, to feel the hurt and process the regret and guilt – and when the intensity of sadness is profound – to fully grieve. Remember the power of optimistic cognitive appraisal, where your own experience tells you clearly that in dealing with difficult situations in the past, you can now see the positive results nestled within apparently negative life events. The blessing sleeps next to the wound.

When sadness is particularly prolonged, intense,

and focused on a specific loss – death of a loved one, divorce, loss of a job, or significant functional disability through injury or illness – it transforms into the more complex brew of grief. The initial stage is characterized by disbelief and denial, along with varying degrees of alarm and arousal, or shock and numbing. As it moves into a more acute phase, there is crying, intense feelings of despair, anger, and fears of additional loss. There may be uncontrollable yearnings for the loss to be retrieved, or searching for a person in shared familiar places or dreams, with seemingly constant reminders everywhere. Anger may be displaced onto others in the form of blame, or jealousy of those who seem happy and do not, at first glance, appear to have significant struggles.

You may take on a heavy load of guilt, a staggering pile of regrets and "if only" grievances against yourself, the heaviness of all you should or would or could have done differently. The helpless, powerless sense of loss of control can be overwhelming. As grief gradually subsides, there may be the sensation of no longer being miserable, just empty, which is actually great progress. You have depleted yourself by excavating closer to the bottom of the sorrow, and now there is nothing left down in that well. Eventually, hope returns and there is renewed energy to re-establish routines, reorganize one's life and reinvent dreams. Reflective time, ceremony and ritual can be most helpful here to reintegrate the new you, as you slowly smile and laugh again, without feeling you are being unfaithful to the memories of your loss.

Now Go Deeper
Choose an experience that caused great grief for you.
Draw or collage its contours and depths. See what
there still may be to heal.

Initially, grief always disorients and overwhelms.
The inner workings of melancholy remind you that
one never "gets over" difficult experiences, but you
can somehow fit them into the fabric of the big picture of your life. Grief cycles, and past losses may
unexpectedly arise when least expected. Grieving –
the natural outcome when love is combined with loss
– arises from an accumulation of feelings requiring
you to slow down and surrender to it, allowing you to
build the capacity for resiliency. When you open to
your grief, and reconcile it with the facts of your life,
you may temporarily enter into the blue of nothing-
ness. Embracing this process is more a marathon than
a sprint. You can remain radiant in your melancholy.
Your shining allows others to do the same—and the
world is constantly blessed by the presence of healed
people. Remember always that even in the most difficult circumstances, there are beautiful moments.
Don't let yesterday take up too much of today.
When you learn to meet your own pain without
aversion, it allows you to be present with another's
distress. There is a continuum of caring, from pity
and sympathy to empathy and compassion. With pity

and sympathy, you are still wrapped up in your emotions, and you try to make others feel better, or fill them with stories to please or distract them, rather than allowing the full expression of *their* emotions. The feeling of empathy involves the capacity to empty the mind, and just be present with your whole being for someone else's emotions and needs—you become a safe container that invites them to experience whatever is welling up. You resonate with understanding their point of view, without judging or attempts to alter it. Giving advice, consoling, educating, interrogating, making judgments or comparisons, or sharing your own version of what occurred, are all barriers to empathy.

Being fully present with their experience, compassion then arises naturally, because you instinctively want to remove suffering by offering them some assistance. Empathy understands feelings, while compassion comprehends needs. Grief has its own rhythms for each person. Just be there, ask the grieving person what they need, and give them what they want if you can. Focus on attentive listening and demonstrative caring: nurture rather than attempt to "fix" anything. Listening involves being spacious and at ease with the refuge of silence, which has its own great healing power. Not the cold stony silence of judgment or comparison, with its waves of unspoken criticism. Not the hard silence of walls of withdrawal. But the warm comforting blanket of simply knowing one is not alone.

70

It is normal and natural for men to cry when they are hurting, emotionally or otherwise. Even if you are just feeling a bit down or melancholy, and not thrashing around in the throes of deep grief, never be ashamed to cry. It is the way for things to get better, the first step. Just allow the body to do what only the body can do. Become familiar with and welcome your tears. Let go of all those years when you could not or would not open yourself to this sweet, healing release. Given how much suffering there is in the world, it is difficult to imagine how most men get through a month without a good cleansing cry.

IX

FORGIVENESS

Forgiveness is a gift you give yourself. It is a soothing balm that allows you to move beyond narratives that dwell on past hurts and limit future possibilities. It is a large, beautiful, buoyant word, a fundamental capacity biologically encoded into human nature. Besides learning how to grieve the inevitable losses that occur in life, understanding and practicing forgiveness is incredibly important. It helps you unravel a story that binds and restricts you. The path of forgiveness asks you to experience fully all the varied emotions jumbled together in the tale of how you were harmed or wronged. To forgive is so difficult because it revisits the original wound, and draws you closer to its source. This is much more demanding than hiding the hurt, or covering it over with positive, syrupy sentiments. Only by revealing and then reimagining your relationship to the wound can it fully heal. To forgive *does not* involve forgetting or condoning hurtful events from the past. It *does* mean not making someone else endlessly responsible for your current wellbeing. Forgiveness recognizes that navigating the way you feel in the present is more important than reviewing and reliving what happened to you historically; that constantly focusing on the past only contributes to current distress.

How much of your emotional real estate is consumed by insisting that your past should somehow change? Perhaps you are afraid of being defenseless, or considered a doormat if you forgive. So often, people make excuses and find justifications for their ongoing hostile positions or actions, which only keeps them locked in a prison of blame and shame. Lack of forgiveness keeps you ruminating on old transgressions, mired in feelings of hostility and resentment toward someone else, which has an adverse impact on *your* physical, mental, spiritual and relational health. Holding onto the negative makes you feel angry, sad, or anxious. When thoughts of the offending person or the situation arise, do you feel peaceful or stressed out? Ask yourself this simple question and you'll identify where you are in terms of letting go. Are you capable of turning grievances into positive stories about your capacity for survival, while reducing or eliminating the chronicles that feed motivations toward revenge? Forgiveness is a form of self-love, because with it you choose to not harbor the pain, to drop constraining regrets and festering resentments, thereby increasing both optimism and physical vitality.

Forgiveness begins in the part of you that was never wounded, before it can take hold at the center of the emotional hurt. Imagine an injury to your physical body. What happens first in the immediate area is all about protection: resources to stop bleeding and mobilize against infection. Then another part of you sends reinforcements, to allow healthy tissue to slowly regenerate. Your body sets up optimal conditions in which healing might occur, including increasing the blood supply of vital nutrients, and sloughing off dead tissue. So you first also build walls, or try to escape in various ways, to shield yourself from the emotional trauma enveloping you. Then it becomes possible to accept support from loved ones; you begin to shed old painful memories by giving yourself permission to feel absolutely everything associated with them, rather than burying the more painful aspects. Grieving well provides the fertile conditions in which forgiveness might eventually heal the hurt. The scars may always be there, but forgiveness allows them to not fester, thus demanding less of your energy and attention over time.

How do you actually begin to forgive someone who frustrated, hurt, controlled or abandoned you, or did not recognize, respect or respond to you? Untangling yourself from the aversions, reactions, judgments, and strident storytelling involves softening the sense of other as enemy. It is hard to give up grievances toward people you believe have wronged you. If you can't blame your misery and touchiness on them, then you have to take full responsibility for yourself. Until you can see the enemy as someone who can teach you, your work is not done. No need to invite them to lunch, but the willingness to see their wounds – and to feel the weight of their guilt and burden – enables your own empathy. Forgiveness is not pity for the offending perpetrator, but rather an acknowledgement of shared humanity, even in the most heinous of circumstances. I have found that it takes two to tango, but only one to initiate steps toward forgiveness. Release all the negative feelings and punishing demands. Check in with your body to see if there is anything you are holding back, if something is blocking the process. Whether you communicate forgiveness directly in the presence of the other, or not, your own internal sense of release and peace is the reward.

A piece of this process always involves absolving yourself of any wrongdoing, real or imagined. As with grieving, self-forgiveness asks you to deeply examine any regrets or guilt you are clutching as part of the story around a particular event. The essence of a regret is an emotional rewind, variations on the theme of "I wish." You experience distress over unfulfilled desires; perhaps a different choice would have produced a better outcome. You *inadvertently* caused pain or harm, perceived or real, to someone or yourself, and you wish you could change the past. What distinguishes guilt from regret is the addition of harsh self-criticism. It arises because you believe that you have *intentionally* done, or not done, something that caused another harm or pain in some way. It is a feeling of responsibility for some offense or wrong, whether real or imagined—acting like a stirring slumbering snake demanding to be fed. When you label yourself as stupid, worthless, or bad for having made a mistake, you add heavy guilt and self-reproach to the weight of a simple regret. You may also feel guilty because you violated your own values or ethical code—by cheating or stealing, lying to others or to yourself, or when your actual behavior does not live up to your lofty intention. You smoke, drink, or overeat, despite promises to the contrary. Guilt can also arise from hidden "unacceptable" desires, or even from not helping others enough. Survival guilt can consume you because you did not die while others did—in war, a cancer battle, a car crash or natural disaster.

Guilt is a thief, intent on robbing you of inner tranquility. While it focuses on behavior, its sidekick, shame, places its laser focus on the core of your being: not only did you do something wrong, but *you* are wrong, flawed. Shame thrives in secrecy, silence and judgment. Observe and stay attuned to what guilt and shame have to say, deeply contemplate the lessons, but then let go. Self-forgiveness is an essential ingredient of forgiving someone else, a skill that is akin to hugging yourself, allowing its healing light to offer new possibilities for peace and prosperity. Realize that your own pain is the doorway to understanding the suffering of others. To forgive yourself means to give yourself permission to be human; to have limitations, to be a source of pain and disappointment to others, to learn often by making mistakes, to say things that you wish you hadn't said, to have emotions that arise and are expressed in damaging ways. Once you can forgive yourself, and see the solace in your own imperfections, it is easier to allow other people to have their blunders too. Try looking into your own eyes at the end of each day with forgiveness for not being perfect, for all those little moments in which you did not live up to your own standards of behavior and being.

Now Go Deeper
Confessional writing can be useful. Explore where you have made mistakes and need to forgive yourself. "I forgive myself for...I forgive myself for judging myself for...I forgive myself for forgetting...I forgive myself for believing..."

Lack of forgiveness is the mortar in the walls that keep you stuck and seal your heart shut. The fortifications become stronger and harder over time, constraining your very life force. Forgive yourself anytime for anything. Confess, apologize and make reparations to yourself. Consciously practice with small things, like keys locked in the car, forgotten shopping lists, the burst of anger, and the things you said while blinded by it. Forgiveness is often about less effort, and more surrender to its healing process. To just relax and allow, and release the struggle, is often the most difficult path of all. It asks you to dissolve into, rather than wrestle against. Find the ease within the effort. Forgiveness, like appreciation and compassion, is a natural expression of your humanity. Practicing makes it simpler to find. It is eternal and ever available—not a quick-fix decision, but a determined process. Let go of the crushing burden of guilt, and liberate yourself from the bondage of past acts.

X

SOLITUDE AND FRIENDSHIP

Being lonely and being alone are not the same experience. Loneliness is about not feeling connected, despite the desire to do so—a familiar café where fear and sadness are often your only companions, their voices echoing loudly in the emptiness. Solitude is connecting to yourself, entering into the depths of your own inner world, where eternity stretches before you, spacious and welcoming. Whereas loneliness exposes you to the raw fragility of human existence, solitude is instead choosing to wrap yourself in a warm nurturing cocoon. It can be enhanced by a specific physical location, or a state of mind, an internally focused sensibility in the midst of a crowd. This unique landscape invites you to just be, and to touch the fertile soil of yearning and recollections, where the seeds of your destiny await your attention, before they can manifest in the external world. It is a great garden of silence, pregnant with potential. There you will find both struggle and peace, just as in the outer plane of existence. But you must claim this far-distant inner realm, which will never leave you, in order to truly make it your own. Whenever and wherever you might access it, you come home – again and again – to the beating of your own heart.

Time alone, in which you can be curious and question everything, is the only true way to get to know oneself. Solitude allows a different kind of seeing: what is hidden, covered, trapped, as well as what lurks inside that needs to be released. Being lost in thought, and in no thought at all. It teaches you to drop the weight of your musings, and sing like a solitary bird in a receptive and accepting forest, where prayer, study, meditation, retreat, and ritual set the stage for both insight and compassionate action. When you take a spell away from the daily race, quiet the turbulence of your normal pace, and slow down to the speed of life, you stimulate different parts of you. You open to new ideas, and attune yourself more deeply to what you really love. The sense of spaciousness to just be, in a world so consumed by doing, is good for you on every level. When combined with being outside and connecting with the intricacies of the planet, it is powerful elixir indeed, aligning your self with the very rhythms of life. You stop and resonate with the primal beat underlying normal everyday existence. Such fine-tuning gradually brings inner and outer life into harmony.

Welcome the gifts of solitude and establish a sanctuary for yourself, a place where you can always go to take refuge, refresh your spirit, and regain your strength. What places and practices always welcome you back, like the shade of a tree where you might rest and feel safe? Everyone needs a sanctuary, yet few take time to create one. Many people have favorite spots in the natural external world they enjoy visiting, where they revitalize themselves: a garden, beach or forest path. For others it might be a city sculpture garden, a cozy library nook, or a tranquil café. A pen, a journal and a quiet place suffice—they are all the inner gizmo gear you need. Turn off everything else! You can also use your creative imagination to build and enjoy an inner haven that is extremely calming and empowering. The setting and overall structure are changeable and located anywhere, with any special elements or chambers you might want to conceive. Perhaps there is a waterfall feature, where you can allow whatever quality you need at the moment to penetrate every cell of your being. Maybe there is a transporter allowing you to visit special locales, a real-life screen to replay various parts of your life, a costume closet – each disguise carrying its own special superpower – a healing grotto, a wisdom altar, a gazebo where various guides come to offer advice on dilemmas. You are both architect and interior designer, determining how grand and elaborate, or little and cozy. Your sanctuary – inner, outer, or a combination of both – is your own personalized private enclave of possibility.

The great societal lie is that, in your quest to be

independent, you have to do it all on your own. The reality is that you have to do it yourself, and you can't do it alone. The social nature of life is a deep-seated human value, and everyone craves connection through compliments in the wonderful moments, and compassion in the more challenging ones. The bonds of friendship, invisible loving threads, extend through life's journey, nurturing through storms and sunshine alike. Build and enjoy great friendships, seek out excellent people – beyond kin and kith – who contribute to your vitality and your capacity for growth. Good friends deepen the value and meaning of life, and best friends know the song of your heart, and can sing it back to you when you forget. They consistently show up and stand with you.

What qualities do you value most in a friend-ship—integrity, enthusiasm, humor, positive atti-tude, dependability? Trust between friends develops over time, through increasing openness and intimate sharing. Its foundation is built through mutual re-spect, vulnerability and honesty. A good friend is someone with whom you can be your authentic self, with whom there is no need for masks or mirrors. You share the rarified air of radical honesty, the mu-sic of your own truth telling takes wing, and voices sing with sincerity. Your own perception of your ac-tions may be filled with illusions. Kindred spirits can provide feedback, reflect back on what they observe, helping you to see your blind spots and shadow out-lines. The profound communion of friendship is an endearing counterpoint to your essential capacity for solitude. The joy of meeting and the sorrow of separation are both gifts; friendship offers the chance to embrace with gratitude all the sweetness or bitterness, as the case may be. This existence seems so fragile at times, and the tender trembling of a friend's caring is extraordinary.

Now Go Deeper
Who do you consider your best friends and why?

Love yourself enough to find a mentor or guide — someone who has been where you want to go, and can offer sound advice for that specific journey. Beyond coach or instructor, the mentor relationship is a much more intense student-teacher interaction, a person who actively pushes you to enhance your skills. A mentor may use her influence to further your advancement, or offer counsel in discouraging times. A mentor inspires your inner dream by who they are, how they live, or what they have accomplished— a wizard who might illuminate and expand your view of the universe. Most elders are honored to have a chance to pass on their wisdom, to share their expertise, and to contribute to the unfolding of a younger man's potential. You lose nothing by sincerely asking, and have much to gain when the response is a resounding yes. Think big and create your own dream team of supportive individuals to magnify your success. Who you know is often as important as what you know in achieving results.

Bestow upon yourself the gift of finding your own tribe, your special crew, and create a band of brothers and sisters who will not only celebrate your successes, but also support you in challenging times, helping you discover more of who you really are. Every man wants to be appreciated for who he is, and to contribute in some way to the greater whole. As groups of friends openly share together their individual journeys to become more aware, they are gifted with highly nurturing moments of deep affection, sweet connection, and the magical brew of laughter and tears. Establish regular contact with others with whom you feel kinship, a certain inexplicable bonding, a resonance that seems natural and easy. This breaks you out of the isolation that engulfs so many men. Just start with one or two friends, and go from there to form a group that meets regularly to discuss what really matters in this life. Not politics or sports, but your most intimate dreams and passions, the landscape of your struggles and stuck places.

Standing shoulder-to-shoulder regularly with other men has increased my listening skills, my ability to be present and open, and has helped me to work through some of my issues—qualities that have tremendously enhanced intimacy with my partner. You enter new territory as a man, where the joys of a truly empowered community await you. Learn to dance between going within and reaching out, to offer support, but also to request and receive it into your life.

The world needs you to be yourself, to simultaneously own your uniqueness and fully inhabit your ties to your fellow human beings. Be both monkish in your solitude and gregarious in your myriad connections. Become well versed in the fine art of friendship. An old tribal proverb remembers that shared joy is double joy, and shared sorrow is half sorrow.

XI

SEXUALITY

You have been fed a great lie: sex is dirty, save it for the one you love. What an absurd view, and yet, if you dig deeply, you may find some of this crazy belief system within you. Your impetuous primeval urges of lust, intoxication and restlessness need always to be honored. That does not mean that you have to act on every desire, but sexual exploration is part of being vital. As long as there is honesty, safety, kindness and mutual consent, there is no harm in enjoying the delight of sharing your body with another. The gifts of sensual and sexual pleasure your body offers are exquisite. Each man must decide for himself – beyond the noisy mob groupthink definitions of "normal" – what is fulfilling and meaningful for him in terms of his sexual expression. Many men have discovered that the "hook up" culture is ultimately unfulfilling, that it is more interesting –though scarier – to explore the slowly unfolding intricacies of intimacy, than the temporary excitement of the hunt.

Most of us have been subjected to various foolish falsehoods about sexuality:

As a man, you must be ready and available for sex at any time. The reality is every man has their own individual conditions that help them feel relaxed, connected and comfortable in a sexual encounter. To declare that they should be able to "get it up" under any circumstance is ridiculous. I secretly suffered for a few years in my twenties, never knowing when impotence might render me confused, upset, and unable to "perform." My penis wasn't cooperating because my heart wasn't in the encounter—feedback I was unable to appreciate at the time.

Sex is best when natural and spontaneous. This untruth implies that there is nothing to learn in order to be a good lover. So you probably were never directly taught the basics about how male and female bodies work, in terms of genital anatomy and the physiology of sexual pleasure.

The sexual experience is a performance, orchestrated by the dominant man, and the grand finale is always orgasm. This denies the whole spectrum of sensual pleasure available, and focuses only on orgasm-oriented achievement. Sounds more like work than a mutually satisfying exchange. Do you really watch a sunset just for the moment the sun goes down? You can kiss, hug, massage, touch, fondle, bite, rub, wrestle, dance erotically, or watch each other while you touch yourselves.

Some men have sex with women, some with men,

some with both women and men. Many different religious followers have created rules, which they then attribute to the will of some divine being, to label various forms of sexual expression as wrong, placing restrictions on what is acceptable or not. As a result, the number of both men and women in the world who find themselves incapable or inhibited about giving or receiving sexual pleasure is enormous. So much suffering is created because of the destructive idea that to be a moral and good person one must suppress, repress or deny the pleasures of the body! Clearly, rape and pedophilia – both more about "power over" than sexuality – are unacceptable, violent expressions, because by definition, mutual conscious consent is missing. Getting someone drunk or high, or threatening or manipulating them so you get them to have sex with you also fits in this category. What other aspects of sexual expression are not okay for you? The pursuit of three short squirts can be life affirming – or destructive – for both yourself and others you encounter. Learn to make good choices.

Many times, feeling horny is just feedback that your body needs some touching and holding. Experiment with sensing what your real desire is, whether just physical contact or something more. Men tend to sexualize many of their needs—especially for touch, connection, discharge of unpleasant feelings, and release of tension. Tuning into your sexual and sensual flows throughout the day is another essential aspect of knowing yourself. Pamper your body, and explore purely *sensual* pleasure, examining where it might shift into *sexual*. Sharing massage or food with another can help you to discover this boundary. Investigate the subtle sexual energy of flirting. Ask your partner what they would like. Look them in the eyes while sharing pleasures. Orgasm and ejaculation are two distinct phenomena. Beyond the male and female G spots, learn to practice tantric sex, and to circulate this precious energy within your body. Explore the BDSM world, and your own private fantasies.

Now Go Deeper

Identify three sensual or sexual experiences you would like to explore, distinguishing between these two different energies.

Is sex with no heart or emotions involved what you authentically desire? Most porn does not demonstrate – nor promote – the qualities of a sensitive, sensual, passionate, attentive, nurturing, imaginative male lover. The habit of porn can bombard you with images, invading your mind throughout the day, and even while lovemaking, which take you away from being present with your partner. What might you be doing instead of watching porn? Do you regularly use it as an escape when feeling lonely or unmotivated, a secret that separates you from your beloved? Porn may help you safely explore what kinks bring delight, and can serve as enjoyable fantasy release. Is it something you might share together with your partner? Educate yourself about the double life of a sex addict, whose unhealthy relationship with this precious energy degrades their entire life. The porn influenced mainstream culture transmits all sorts of colluding messages, where young girls get repeated conditioning that to be worthy of love, they have to be like a porn star, in terms of body, dress and behaviors. Given the downside, does it really agree with your wellbeing? Every man must find a healthy and life affirming path through all the mindless sexual stimulation that is constantly available.

If an adult wanted to make money through prostitution, why not allow that to occur in a safe, legal environment? Realizing that this person is someone else's daughter or son might change your perspective, especially if you already have children. Is whatever men find arousing okay? Do sex workers have no option but to comply since they are receiving money? Will it ever be possible to stop childhood sexual abuse, rape and battery when the objectification of women inherent in both porn and prostitution is encouraged and accepted? Deciding where you stand on these issues is to step into the morass of the collective archetypal male shadow—the history of male domination, repression and oppression of those deemed "lesser than." Based on your own deeply held values, what is okay for you? Pole dancing, humiliating jokes about women, catcalls – whistling or lewd comments – to a passing female, occasional forays into porn, paying someone for sex if you are "kind" or "respectful?"

I am a Sicilian-American (white) straight male, who has learned a few things along the way about our gay brothers. Homophobia is a fear-based dislike of homosexual people, which can manifest in prejudice and violence. If you have some belief that homosexual sexual activities are disgusting or not natural, then do not engage in those practices. Why does it have to become you against them, when respect and tolerance are just as easy to embrace? Many people come out during their teenage years, a time of accelerated learning about sexual identity, though later in life may feel safer for some to acknowledge being lesbian, gay, bisexual, transgender, queer, intersex, or asexual (LGBTQIA). The process happens in different ways for different people. Coming out does not mean you tell everybody; better to first choose carefully those who are more likely to react positively and be supportive. If you are a straight man, you really have no clue, unless a gay family member or friend has invited you in to support them. I know from experience that when gay and straight men openly share what separates and connects them, the world is richer.

Sexual connection can be a healing balm, a shelter that comforts and opens, transforming the dark places of unworthiness in each other. It can also be a source of great suffering and unfulfilled desire. Navigating the pleasure and pain of sexuality requires attention, awareness, and your willingness to constantly explore and open yourself. Hot monogamy is possible, and the fullness and radiance of the delights of wild spontaneity can be preserved over time. Or maybe your tendencies and commitments are more exploratory, and multiple partners, or an open sexual partnership, hold more appeal. Polyamory emphasizes that is possible to be romantically involved, in love, and sexual with multiple people at the same time. The important and essential aspect is that you tell the truth and keep your agreements — not easy in a culture where having deleterious secret affairs is common. You get to decide as an adult how to inhabit your own body, and in what ways you express your sexuality, including pleasuring yourself alone. You can transform the skewed perspectives and faulty conditioning you received from family, religious institutions, and the culture in general. As with other aspects of your journey, you create – and hopefully live– *your* values, share experiences and insights with close friends, and drop whatever seems meaningless or not part of your truest self. Be patient as the flower of your authentic sexuality gradually opens, for it can never be forced.

XII

LOVE

Love is such a basic human need; no wonder the word remains so much a part of the daily lexicon, suffering from an embarrassment of meanings. Many philosophers and spiritual paths have attempted to define its essence, and such a treatise is beyond the scope of this small tome. However, it is clear that love involves intimate connection and acceptance, rooted in giving that which you seek. In the primal conversation of togetherness, you discover each other's beauty. Love is most certainly not something that strikes like Cupid's arrow – a state you just fall into, an easily indulged sentiment – but rather an art and skill requiring practice like any other worthy human pursuit. There is a psychological notion called the *imago*, the essence of which is that you will be attracted to people who embody both the best and the worst key characteristics of the people who raised you. These potential partners may also exhibit essential aspects of your lost self, the parts that went underground in your childhood, because it was not safe to express them. Essentially, in your search for a mate you will be attracted to people that in some ways re-create conditions of your childhood. A part of you always wants to heal hidden hurts. You unconsciously choose adult intimate relationships that offer you similar conditions from the past, but in a present where you are more empowered to deal with them skillfully. Love is a great laboratory for healing and awakening, serving as both crucible and sanctuary, offering both rupture and radiance.

When you first encounter someone you're attracted to, it is inevitable that a fair amount of projection will occur as part of the intoxication between you. Lost in the early pheromone fog of incipient lust, it is difficult to really see the other—and so you imagine, quite pleasurably, that they will fill the hole in your soul, lift the darkened veil from your spirit, be the answer to all your dreams. You fill in the blanks, so to speak, of your knowledge of who this person really is, with those qualities you would really like them to possess. Over time, this house of cards often comes tumbling down as you come to truly know each other. Gradually you see more clearly their faults and limitations, and decide you are capable of accepting them, or that there is just not a compatible fit for the various relationship puzzle parts. Staying in a relationship, in the hopes that the other will magically change in very fundamental ways, is a prescription for unhappiness. You can transform yourself, and you can support and encourage positive shifts in the other, but you cannot count on specific qualities changing to meet your expectations. So get clear from the beginning on the red flags that really matter.

For many years, my *modus operandi* (MO) in relationships was: "I am Mr. Bodhisattva, and I am here to help you heal, with no selfish requirements of my own." Only when I let that go – and learned to ask for what I needed – was I able to engage in a loving partnership, without one foot always out the door. I still have to really stay awake, because it is so easy to fall into old patterns of pleasing in order to be liked, while ignoring my own needs—or even the reality that I have any!

Now Go Deeper
What is your usual MO in an intimate relationship? How do you present yourself?

Affectionate acceptance implies a commitment to kindness, even in the face of challenging moments. Glances, touches, and whispers, embroidered with reverence and patience, are the weft of its fine weave. It also means that you have a basic compatibility in how much connection and physical affection feels good to each of you. If your notion is to get together twice a week with little contact in between, and your current romantic interest wants to talk three times a day and spend five nights together, then there is not a match in a very fundamental way. Acceptance involves a mindset free of judgments and the belief that your way is the only right one. You may both have different needs in terms of the quality and quantity of expressed affection and appreciation. Explore each other's unique language of love.

Benevolent boundaries involve a healthy sense, for both of you, of what to reveal versus what to conceal about your own inner workings: beliefs, thoughts, feelings, deep desires, choices, and experiences. You are also clear about your yes, no and maybe, in terms of what you are willing to do for the other. There is an important distinction between having a giving generosity of spirit, versus the habit of people pleasing. Co-dependency occurs when you put more time and energy into thinking about and doing for the other than yourself. Getting sucked into a partner's bad mood, or assuming something is your fault when things go wrong, does not facilitate healthy connections. When you have good boundaries, you acknowledge the reality of competing desires—to please others, and to take good care of yourself. You are aware of your own needs and preferences, and you can make requests—asking amiably for support or what you'd like to be different.

Requests are specific invitations: "would you be willing to" respectfully asserts a need or want, and allows for a variety of responses including no, maybe, or not now. They are devoid of guilt trips and criticism, and don't try to change or control the other in order to get your way—the opposite of "should" or "supposed to." Requests connect, demands push away. Boundaries are dynamic and flexible. You liberate yourself from the tyranny of others' judgments. You allow others to have their own experience—without jumping in to fix or rescue. Signs of healthy boundaries include a sense of spaciousness in the relationship, and the ability to make requests with kindness, without emotional charge. You can be assertive, without being aggressive. Boundaries are where the core issue of any relationship will keep showing up. Some of your deepest childhood wounds occurred because of unhealthy boundaries. Creating healthy ones with your partner in the present heals what you were unable to do in the past, because you were only a child—keep out what was unwanted, or ask for what you needed.

The ability to discuss anything and everything that arises is facilitated by conscious communication. The focus is on determining and sharing what each person is feeling and needing, rather than assigning blame or pointing fingers. Responsibility is to be taken not assigned. It also means that you do not believe everything you think as absolute truth, that you are willing to inquire about a misunderstanding rather than ignore it, realizing that what you heard may not be what they actually said. Conflict is a normal part of any relationship. Always first look inside yourself to find the breakdown, rather than mindlessly blaming the other. Be smart about choosing a time when both of you are in a good space to discuss sensitive issues. End of the day, being hungry, tired, rushed, hot or cold, makes anyone more irritable. Negative moods can be contagious. Learn to share what is really bothering you in a few words. Sometimes all a partner wants is to be heard, often difficult for men who are more comfortable with the find-a-solution approach. Listen with a desire to understand, rather than to reply. Listen to discover the other's loving intent behind what they are saying. Listen for the good in one another. Empathy first, then advice if wanted; showing empathy doesn't mean you agree or that you're obligated to do anything different. It just means you "get it." It is about *being with*, rather than jumping into fix-it mode.

Create safety by agreeing to take a time out when emotions or voices start rising, when active listening and problem-solving abilities have vanished. Dialing back the intensity, feeling secure and understood often helps people feel stronger, or see new solutions. It is hard to keep your heart open with someone who is intent on making you wrong. When you most want to run is when you most need to stay. And, men often need their cave and time alone to process their emotions and get clear—important for your mate to understand. Whatever the conflict, it can be worked with and worked through. Learn to savor the good in a bad relationship day—by keeping yourself open and vulnerable despite the difficulties, and turning towards the conflict rather than avoiding it. When, in order to minimize conflict, you stop being honest and consistently lose your voice, resentments build and trust erodes—both destructive forces to love and intimacy. And it is helpful – solution rather than blame oriented – to remember the principles of Right Speech: is what you are about to share true, kind, and necessary? So greet those clashing, challenging moments of disagreement with the larger conscious perspective that they can be compost that nourishes the garden of your connection.

XIII

FATHERHOOD

Hopefully you enter this magical realm by conscious choice, rather than through unintended consequence. Becoming a father is less about biology than about showing up, since you may find yourself parenting the children of another man, perhaps because of your love for their mother. Or you may partner with a man and adopt or also father his children. The journey of healthy fatherhood begins with the awareness that this is a life changing process. Ideally, you already have significant grounding and comfort in your own body, gender, sexuality, and relation to the world. You don't have to have all the answers, but you need to be a willing pupil. You will have to learn a whole new set of communication skills, as your offspring passes from *babydom* through *teenhood* and beyond. Understand that in the coming years, your children will not need you the same way they need you now — a disheartening and exciting reality. And because each child is a unique personality, you must discover and accommodate to their style of relating and learning. Adjust and adapt! Being a father calls forth from deep within you illuminating qualities you did not imagine you possessed.

Fatherhood brings some clarity to your relationship with your own father. What my father did or didn't do greatly influenced my own knowledge, attitudes, feelings and behaviors as a dad. I found myself examining what lessons he gave, and how I expressed these qualities in my daily life as a parent. If your experiences are similar to mine, the negative ways you perceive you are like your father will become magnified, as you strive to do your best with your own children, and not repeat what you consider his mistakes. What do you most want from him now, as you create your own path of being a father? The more you have examined his gifts and wounds to you, the more likely you will find a way to pass on the best to your own children.

Now Go Deeper
What specific gifts from your dad do you want to pass on to your children, or other young men?

While not universally true, fathering tends to be different than mothering — and each provides something the emerging individual needs. The daddy dynamic means that you are likely to be more assertively active with your children, offering new exciting pastimes — everything from your body as jungle gym, to sports and challenging outdoor activities. While mothers tend to cushion their baby from distress and irritations, dads are more likely to bring them to the edge, helping them to "stretch" emotionally and physically. Your different approach can help manage frustration, persist in problem solving, and explore new activities and places. Reading your moods through tone of voice, facial expressions, and other nonverbal cues instructs them on the finer nuances of emotional communication. Balanced daily interactions offer comfort and security, as well as fun and excitement. The fathering challenge is maintaining a level of stimulation that keeps your child engaged, without pushing them too far.

Newborns are prepared by millions of years of genetic memory to manipulate their environment to ensure survival. They are also a catalyst for you, the father, to change your life. You and your baby are meant to grow together—a driving force of evolution is the interaction of parents with their young. What a journey from carefree bachelor who can drop their undies wherever they fall, to a father picking up someone else's toys! Most men of this era do not have much prior experience with babies. Life before children can seem a very far away land indeed. Being a new father often creates anxieties, frustrations and fears. You may be jealous of the time baby spends with mom, and envious of her "natural" parenting ways. I found that taking a walk with the babe in a chest pack, or having them sleep nestled on my body was captivating beyond belief. My infant daughters' smells and warm aliveness generated a deep sense of bonded connection. Early on, I recommend that you take care of your newborn entirely on your own for certain times and activities. Creating "fathering space" builds your confidence and hones your parenting skills, empathy, and emotional depth from the get-go.

I invite you to ponder these additional thoughts and see if they ring true.

The present of your presence is profound. Prioritize being fully present with your children, and gift them your time, a great bounty beyond what you might provide materially for their betterment.

Listening to your children affirms them. Demonstrate by actively listening that you are interested in their ideas, interests and concerns.

Affection deepens attachment. There are many languages of love, from cooking a favorite meal to surprising with small gifts, from verbal accolades to warm embraces, from a sweet note for something well done, to just being with them when they are disappointed. Learn them all. You are filling the well of love your children will drink from for the rest of their lives.

Play enhances essential coping skills. Read to them, make up games, and get outside in nature. Limit screen time and champion eating together without other distractions. At every stage of development, but especially during the early years, their abundant imagination can stimulate your own.

They are your teachers. Honor their ability to effort-lessly remind you of what is most important, some of which is easily forgotten in the everyday demands of adulthood. They will test your kindness and your pa-tience in innumerable, unimaginable ways. And they will make you smile and laugh as never before.

Gentle discipline guides. Everyone makes mis-takes! Discipline is not about punishment, but conse-quences for not keeping agreements. Setting limits, guiding and judiciously giving feedback can be done with love. Learn how to offer correction and direc-tion without creating resentment.

Positive role modeling is powerful. "Do as I say, not as I do," is great hypocrisy. Modeling – being a living example – is worth more to your children than anything you could ever tell them. "I don't know," and "I apologize," are some of the most empowering words a parent can utter.

Sometimes, the primary adults raising a child have very diverse parenting notions and abilities—and the children are wounded on that battlefield. Still mar-ried, never married, divorced, parenting with another, or fathering with another man, showing respect and remaining supportive for the other parent reinforces that the children are neither an emotional dumping ground, nor a pawn in seemingly endless parental conflicts. Respect for another does not necessarily mean we agree with their choices or opinions, yet we honor the reality that they are a sentient being, who deserves our kindness and caring—treating with reverence their very existence, because of – and in spite of – their imperfections. Children suffer most from a divorce when the father disappears, or there is ongoing hostility between the parents. Don't become a deadbeat dad, a Disneyland dad or a nowhere dad. No matter the challenges with the other partner, you will be a successful father whenever you are affectionate, attentive to their needs, actively engaged, accepting, and available emotionally. In fact, should you choose to not directly engage in fathering, these qualities are worth remembering in other interactions you have with boys and young men, many of whom suffer from a deep "father hunger."

Like the toddler – but capable of greater destructive actions – the adolescent's job is to declare their independence and push the parents away. They may become "parent deaf" with monosyllabic responses as their main form of communication. This is when you need to call in the resiliency reinforcements. Who are the three to five other caring adults in your adolescent's life that might offer advice that is more likely to be received and considered, since it is not coming from you? It is essential that you foster such relationships for your children while they are younger. Large extended family life—the embrace of many uncles, aunts, cousins, godparents and grandparents—provided this safety net naturally, but the common nuclear family environs demand that you reach out for such assistance. The young ones who best traverse the perils of adolescence experience both a high level of monitoring by their parents, and high levels of affection.

Folklore states that each being has a name assigned to them by the moon and stars, the light of their twinkling yearnings and their flashing failures. To be a father is to illuminate the trail of your child's own name, so they will remain true to it as they age; to realize that our children seek a fuller and farther vision of who they want to be, beyond the limits of our own imaginings. You will always be a father. The time, energy and intensity involved will shift as your children walk their own path. Especially if you have been trustworthy, they will seek your encouragement and counsel as they cross the thresholds of education, career, partnering, and their own parenting.

XIV

DESIRE

One of the most astonishing things about human life is its swiftness, this brief passage of time in which you get to evolve on your profound pilgrimage of discovery. Your mind will always generate more desires than you will have sufficient time and energy to bring forth into reality. Take a front row seat to observe your own desires on intimate terms.

Realize that needs and desires are entirely different beasts. Needs represent the basic requirements for sustaining life. They involve necessities like air, food, water, sleep, and some protection from the elements, including garments and shelter, access to health care and medicine. Humans also have emotional needs for safety, identity, connection, participation, cooperation and contribution, as well as mental exercise needs for creative expression, following curiosity, and learning new skills. Spiritual needs also exist: to connect with the Great Mystery, to make some sense of the meaning and purpose of your life, and to continue evolving and developing. Your brain is engineered for survival, and you are always seeking to get your needs met. If you don't do it consciously, it will find a way to do it unconsciously.

Wants are a whole category of desires, which might be better termed cravings: for various types of pleasure, for material objects, recognition and attention from others, for power and money. Wants are so woven into the fabric of your daily life that they often become invisible. And such cravings are also the source of *samsara*, the endless thirst for sensual pleasures, the fever of longing for more and different. The double-edged sword of craving is that it can lead to unfettered accumulation, greed, addictions, and chronic dissatisfaction. Ultimately, even satisfied wants may not be fulfilling, and can lead to unwholesome behaviors. Their demands can also blind you to all the blessings already constantly falling upon you. For this type of desire, satiety is usually an elusive dream, because "more" is a vortex that easily traps you. This is not to say that such longings are not to be explored for the lessons they teach you, but it helps to always be mindful of the inherent dangers. The craving trap suggests that "there" is always better than "here." When you arrive "there," you will simply generate another want that will look better than "here." You can see this in your own life when you hanker for a particular object that you then succeed in obtaining. The magic and energy of all that yearning soon dissipates, and another object of desire appears on the horizon. The antidote to these cravings is to practice being easily satisfied.

Preferences are the priorities in your morass of wants. They speak to basic rhythms, satisfying habits, the kind of place and personal environment where you enjoy living. They are often rooted physiologically—you are a morning person, you feel better when you eat a certain diet. Such inherent inclinations express your personality—you are extroverted and prefer big parties, you are an external processor who likes to talk a lot, you are a seven on the Enneagram with a tendency to dabble in different things. They reveal themselves in relationship: you are a fuser and enjoy spending a lot of social time with one person, you are attracted to thin body types, you get on easily with water signs. They manifest in activities you enjoy: biking, watching sci-fi movies, live jazz. Preferences emerge as you explore and discover your most basic tendencies.

There is another set of desires that live on the shore of avoidance. It is common for humans to want to evade illness, suffering and pain. Just as you seek pleasure, you also shun unpleasant experiences. As already discussed in terms of fear and grief, part of maturing is getting comfortable with uncertainty, and learning to surrender and accept whatever is happening now. As you become more skillful in dealing with challenging conditions, you become more self-confident that you can handle these life experiences, with sufficient support and attentive awareness. This is the harsh reality: beings that are subject to illness, old age and death will experience illness, old age and death. Despite all your desires for it to be otherwise, that includes you.

Many men have a very active fantasy life. Beyond mere sexual fantasy, a fair amount of "future tripping" captures them and steals the present moment. The someday isle (I'll) is a subtle form of being stranded. By imagining a wonderful future, you can flee from a present you would rather not live, or never learned to enjoy as enough. It is true that fantasy can sometimes be a way to keep alive certain dreams, and daydreaming can generate changes you want to make. Yet most fantasy is simply a desire you take no action on; it never gets married to intention in order to manifest. Sometimes by consciously declaring that a certain desire is really just a fantasy, you can create spaciousness and peace. Nothing needs to happen other than to occasionally enjoy it for what it is: a construction of your mind, built with wants and fueled by an urge to escape.

Finally there is the realm I call deep desire—a persistent, irresistible tug on your heart, a secret longing that has been part of you for a long time, perhaps because the seeds were planted in childhood by some event long forgotten. Deep desires reflect those inner aspects of who you really are that have always wanted expression in the outer world. They play a central role in shaping who you are and the narrative of your life, as your identity morphs throughout your personal evolution. Some mysterious energy repeatedly draws you toward a certain endeavor. You can tell it is really important because it keeps showing up in different forms, and surrendering to it just feels right, even though logically it may not make sense. You see this operative when someone appears to suddenly jettison a successful career in order to pursue something unrelated. Or when they reconnect with that long-lost childhood instrument and go at it with an unforeseen intensity. Or take a year off mid-stride to go on a world walkabout, in to order to find oneself again.

Each day, you are dancing with what I term the nine sacred realms of engagement. They all pull at you, gently requesting – and sometimes demanding – your time and energy. You can conceive of them in three interactive clusters. The first consists of **relationships:** family, friends and force for good—your community or service connections. Next comes **wellbeing:** fun, fitness and fortress—caring for your home. The final triad involves **livelihood:** field of endeavor – your current work – finances, and frontier—the edge of what you are interested in pursuing, where deep desire also dwells.

There is a wonderful Hopi word, *koyannysqatsi*, which roughly translates as "life out of balance." Finding and then stabilizing some sort of equipoise in the modern world is an ongoing challenge. You may struggle with meaningful work, making a living, finding time for family and friends, and daily self-care practices. Somehow, in all of that juggling, your nitty-gritty *heartspace* asks that you muster enough energy to pursue your most vital dreams and revere your deepest desires.

Now Go Deeper
Identify and explore the various elements of a deep desire.

What happens when deep desires have gone silent for a time? When this unseen force no longer tugs you toward what you love? Such plateaus might indicate that you are currently fully engaged in a very satisfying and fulfilled life, and there is no need at the moment for additional prodding from your inner depths. Or you may feel lost in a desert of the ordinary and habitual, with no inspiring oasis in sight. Such fallow periods – though they may feel deadening in a disturbing kind of way – are quite necessary to your development, because they are times of integration at a deep level. Activity and stillness are critical aspects of any biological growth, and this is true for your own evolutionary journey. Deep desire is on vacation because you are not yet ready to embrace its summons. Rather than bemoan or berate yourself for a current lack of passionate involvement, simply allow your curiosity full rein. You can just rest in the spaciousness that comes when temporarily adrift.

I firmly believe that the unique gift of deep desires – as opposed to wants or preferences – is that the "goal" is less important than the changes you go through on the way. Thus it is ultimately more satisfying because the "results" do not evaporate once the luster of getting there has worn off—they've become part of you instead! Deep desire will carry you to both exalted ecstasies and your deepest desolation. It is a chariot upon which your creative intelligence can express itself freely. It invites you to dance on the razor's edge of your own growth, to explore a frontier that will both challenge and reward you in many ways. This is why its call must be answered. You may get to choose the timing, but the summons is not something you control. Sanskrit provides more useful terms for this process. *Satyakama* is true desire – in the sense of growth and evolution – and *satyasankalpa* represents the true resolve needed to get you there. What satyakama is now awakening on the edge of your awareness?

XV

PURPOSE

What does it all mean? Those five words represent a universal human query. It whispers to your soul, and begs you to accept the invitation to set off on an adventure to discover the unknown. The search to leave a significant legacy, and contribute to making the world better, is a widespread impulse—despite the apparently intensely superficial lives so many children of modernity embrace. Creating a value-based, meaningful credo to navigate your life can provide a comforting sense of command. Yet in the headiness of high-minded ideals, you may lose a lot of the immediacy of simple experience—seeing with your senses instead of your thoughts, feeling with your heart rather than your philosophy. Let life and destiny guide you, as much as your concepts and intentions of what it should look like. "Get out of your own way" counsels you to exit your head, and get on with living what is right in front of you. Being you is your most authentic mission. If your life is a book, what is the name of the chapter you are currently living?

Underlying your daily life rests the profound foundation of the interconnectedness of all human beings. The food and physical objects that make survival possible and embellish your daily life do not simply appear on a magic tree in your neighborhood. They are grown, harvested, manufactured or created by other people who – like you – are struggling to define themselves, to find a place in the world that is meaningful and has purpose. Can you slow down long enough to cherish this web of relations in which you not only survive, but also thrive? Your purpose involves your unique contributions to this energetic network through sharing your innate talents, and marshaling your passions. Be patient. If you don't know where you are going, you will end up somewhere else. And sometimes the winding, twisting way is more interesting.

Money is a good servant but a poor master. It's not that money is unimportant, rather that other things are *more* important. People with some degree of monetary security are more relaxed and happy up to a certain point, beyond which additional income does not increase one's sense of wellbeing. Approach the *moneysphere* with conscious intent. See how little you really need to live well. Try alternative ways to make it, observe how you spend it, and stay focused on how it can serve rather than imprison you. Read *Money: Master The Game,* or *Rich Dad, Poor Dad,* and *Your Money Or Your Life*—each helps to deconstruct some of your early monetary conditioning. Observe how those around you are trapped or liberated by the quest for more of it. Is corporate slavery really what you want? Examine the downside of *affluenza* and your own entitlement disorder. Ask someone you believe has a healthy sense of abundance to share her or his own unique views on the subject. For sure, avoid the traps of overusing credit cards, living beyond your current means, failing to save for the inevitable rainy day, or getting involved with too-good-to-be-true bad business blunders.

How much is enough? "Just a little more!" is perhaps the most truthful response ever formulated. Obviously, the answer shifts and evolves as you do. A young person traveling solo – indulging their wanderlust and experiencing new cultures, countries and challenges – needs much less monetary support than a new father nest building in a committed relationship. It is human nature to seek, which often involves more: more comfort, pleasure, knowledge, power, insert your favorite addiction here. Some people decide that making money is their true purpose. There are many happy, satisfied, very wealthy people in the world, who are often also quite generous in helping others. If this feels like the right path for you, then go for it, remembering to smell the roses along the trail, and to have some sense of "enough." And recall that success is a larger universe than just a bull's eye of dollars and cents; it is delineated by what you consistently value as a human being, more than being defined by a single moment of achievement. Extreme luxury married to quiet misery – when too much is never enough – is ultimately self-defeating. How do you personally characterize greed, how do you measure the nebulous notion of success?

Right Livelihood is a Buddhist term that encompasses using your talents, being challenged, learning, and furthering personal growth. It offers you the opportunity to work on something you believe needs doing—beyond pay benefits, vacations and security. It narrows the gap between what you dream and what you do, and deeply honors the gifts you have to offer the world, while acknowledging what is required for survival. Right Livelihood discerns that motivation is often temporary, but the inspiration of a calling is permanent. It involves work that contributes to making the world a better place, understanding that in giving there is always receiving. It syncs with experiencing meaning and vitality, the sensation of feeling alive. It connects in a deep way what you value with what you do every day. Beyond the bigger-better-faster-more of prestige and power, it invites you to embody concern for the common good, to discover your unique contribution to the grand experiment of human evolution.

Unlike just a generation ago, where the norm was to work for a single employer for most of one's working career, you will likely explore more than one vocation. While everyone has periods when earning a living is less than satisfying or inspiring, just don't stay stuck. Change the nature of the work, or your relation to it. Shifting your perspective to a mindset of being of service can transform boring or tedious work. Focus on how your particular job contributes to the larger economic web in which we all participate. Always keep your passionate interests alive, even if they must sleep in the closet for a while. Sustain that YAHOO perspective: **Y**ou **A**lways **H**ave **O**ther **O**ptions! As you discover where the juiciness lives, you can then find ways – including further education or specific skill building – to make a career revolving around those interests. Let what inspires and is of service to others lead the way.

Constantly connected to a digital neighborhood, endlessly distracted, lost in the trance of busyness and the cult of productivity, you can easily drift from living on purpose. Everyone needs a center and an edge. Center is home, in every sense of the word. It is all your relations, everything you deeply love, all that nourishes and supports you. Home is also that little happy peaceful place inside, your inner sanctuary. Edge is the territory of development, risk, change and evolution, where deep desires drive you to a path of growth-infused uncertainty. Somehow each day, you manage to navigate the stormy seas between the life you now have, and the one you would like. Stalked by a plethora of choices, you may sense a perpetual "falling short," with so many desires sacrificed on the altar of conformity. I have been there myself, and

I beseech you to not become obsessed with what is missing in your life! Your fantasy life may be a refuge from your present circumstances, but it is also an integral aspect of your metamorphosis. I really want you to grasp this truth: the double life of the one you wish for, and the one that keeps showing up, is a gap to be embraced, not a shameful lack of authenticity to be spurned.

Now Go Deeper
Create a short and simple "my purpose" declaration, based on the values you hold most dear.

Human beings are always searching for meaning, sometimes on a mountaintop, on a pilgrimage, other times online shopping on a computer. It's not so much "follow your heart," but rather teach and transform your heart to fully embrace what makes you thrilled to arise in the morning, and gratified to lie down at night. You are always falling apart and coming together at the same time, waking up into your own true life, understanding it at a different level. Whatever story you have told yourself about your existence so far, is not large enough to hold all that awaits you on your horizon. Celebrate more than self-criticize, take time to meander rather than clockwork manifest, choose to not be a cog in the malicious machinery of society. When you act out of deep personal values – your own center of gravity that consistently anchors you to your greatest self

– and align your everyday goals with a well-defined purpose, you expand your story, and create a sense of being that is more than enough. You have everything you need to enjoy right here and now, unless you are choosing to be controlled by a dead past or an imagined future. You have complete responsibility for everything you experience, since your actions and emotions influence the reactions of those around you. Everything belongs—all that you think, feel, say and do provide the compost for the next stage in your growth.

XVI

BEING STUCK

I can't impress upon you enough this reality: when the outer circle of the world is not giving you the results you want, then it is time to do more inner exploring. At some point, everyone has the experience of feeling stuck in his life. This is a common and very challenging time, when the gap between the life you have, and the one you think you would like to be living, seems enormous. It is a deep sense of constriction, when a self-imposed prison appears to offer no exit. Little seems to be going right, and all the left turns of fate or destiny – or your own creation – appear to be leading you further into the darkness. The whole world seems against you on some level, even those you normally have found to be supportive or on your side. You begin to believe everything you think as absolute truth, magnifying the worst scenarios. And you become so immersed in some old story, that all you want to do is escape from the emotional pain linked to it. The more you try to run, its chains just bind you tighter and tighter. What you are resisting continues persisting! Being stuck means you're not listening to what existence is actually telling you, stubbornly demanding that life comply with your preconceived version.

When you first begin anything – a new sport, dancing, playing an instrument, or learning a language – you enter the humbling territory of being *unconsciously incompetent*. That just means you are not even aware of everything you are not doing correctly. With practical "rules of thumb," disciplined persistence, and productive feedback you begin to grasp some of what is amiss, and become *consciously incompetent*. Further attentive practice leads you to the next level wherein you are *consciously competent*, which feels much better, a definite sense of progress on the path, and a body-based understanding of how to get there. Ultimately you may achieve some degree of *unconscious competence*, where embodied action and flow are more possible. Your brain has created new pathways, and your learning is now expressed with more capacity and facility than ever before. But this progression is filled with crucial plateaus, where it seems no progress is being made. This is the restless, constricted sensation of being stuck. Other than the "tyranny of perfection," being stuck – with its exasperation, disenchantment and apprehension – is the most common reason people give up on whatever it was they were attempting to learn.

Those many moments on your life journey when

the universe is not aligned with your vision can be painful and obstructive. And it can be overwhelming when faced with a big life decision. A new job, the next step in a relationship, moving to a new place, a big health decision, or the leap of committing to be a father. These large choices can bring up lots of fear and unfinished business. Uncertainty accompanies your most dogged attempts at discernment, and the space of not knowing what to do happens so often in life, one imagines everyone would get good at inhabiting it in a relaxed fashion. If you aren't comfortable yet with uncertainty, start by worshiping ambiguity. A really common barrier to life's flow is that most of us repeatedly respond to uncertainty with fear and withdrawal, rather than curiosity and openness.

Intelligence manifests most not when the brain is humming along, but when it gets stuck or puzzled! The initial step in removing an obstacle is to change the belief that there is an obstacle. Remember that challenge and opportunity are positive words, as opposed to "problem." When you mountain bike, if you focus too much on the obstructions you are more likely to hit them; rather move towards open space. Embrace uncertainty as your mentor or guide every time you experience it, and shift your mindset to see your state of confusion as helpful and interesting. Just declare it so. There is a certain amount of cognitive imperialism at work for most people. Do you hold tightly to the idea that you can *think* your way out of every dilemma? To move from *stuckville* to clarity means that you have to be willing to hang out with your confusion for as long as it takes—despite our impatient culture of immediacy. But the drive to "figure it out" often invites a fear-based process of going over something repetitiously, in the hopes that something helpful might emerge from incessant mental thrashing around in a hall of mirrors. This just reinforces the illusion that you have control over a situation, if only you are willing to engage effort long enough.

The only command you really have is to be centered in whatever is happening, to notice when you have drifted away from center, and to return yourself – over and over – to this inner grounding. Decision fatigue can propel you to do nothing or act impulsively—both are attempts to conserve needed energy. Sometimes the rush of quitting, the impulsive instant buzz of cutting loose, the purity of walking away, the finality of no bridges left unburned seems to hold the potent promise of delivery from your current dilemma. But best to avoid the pattern of feeding on future fantasies, living in one place yet dreaming of another, trapped by your latest seductive scheme for true happiness. You might shed your surroundings but not your own skin, and you'll inevitably bring with you all your unskillful habits and unfinished business. Rather than stagnation or impulsive leaps, I have discovered it is more skillful to embrace uncertainty and patience.

"I am stuck and I don't know why," or the ever

132

empowering "I don't know," are good places to continue the inquiry. Once you acknowledge you are indeed stuck, then you are less likely to just give up, empowering you to continue to find a way beyond the doldrums. It is tempting to find a way *out*, in the form of your favorite pattern of escape – sex, drugs, video games, insert yours – but *through* is the more potent direction. Expose your diversionary or procrastination tactics, and your fears of making the wrong choice. Relax and step back from the puzzle that is foxing you, take a break from the mind web you have spun. Contemplative quiet time in a special "getting clear spot" will open you up. Take yourself out of yourself, embrace an eagle eye's view, and get out of Dodge, surrender to the timeless wisdom of "sleeping on it." Be ruthlessly honest about what you really want, rather than just blindly pleasing others, and then articulate any new insights out loud with compelling veracity.

All this truth telling lifts the initial burden of uncertainty and carries you forth. Truth is meant to baffle you, to be mysterious and dangerous and disorienting—you don't know how it will end. Your truth doesn't have to be sold – you needn't convince others of its validity – just told. The momentum will build, enabling you to take a larger perspective of this dilemma, and increasing your confidence in creating the shift. And you may still emerge without much illumination, inhabiting a space of feeling emptier and disappointed with yourself. Getting clear is a process, not a production: welcome uncertainty, center, consider the options, take a break to contemplate, clarify your truth, and repeat the cycle as needed. This is what is meant by the truism "when there are only two apparent choices, always pick the third."

Now Go Deeper
Identify an area where you feel stuck. Write, draw, or creatively collage three aspects that might help bring clarity.

Essentially, being stuck in making big life decisions always asks you to make an internal shift to resolve your fear around one choice or another. It invites you to clarify your stopping and shopping lists: what you need to let go of and stop doing, and what you need to shop for in terms of inner change and specific personal support. Often, the sooner you step up and start creating that change, the way through reveals itself. Then just take the next obvious step. You can't know how the rest of your life will unfold. I find it very helpful to wire it up so I always win. At the choice point, when you have to make a decision, create a scenario in your mind that either way you will experience success, even if that shows up only in the form of some valuable life lessons. Most importantly, realize that the dream of a life without obstacles in an illusion. Your real life is *right now*, the whole enchilada, including all the unfinished business and daily challenges to your wellbeing. The idea is not so much to fix your dilemmas, to finally arrive at some perfect pinnacle, but to become more fully alive, aware, and adaptable. Your life will never be without quandaries. Consider them signposts that lead you to necessary change. Mine your life deeply, just as it is, with all its wild imperfections.

XVII

HABITS AND INTENTION

The quality of your daily life is ultimately determined by your intentions, and the habits that champion them. A habit is a settled tendency or practice, especially one that is difficult to give up. It is a routine or behavior that is repeated regularly and tends to occur unconsciously and automatically. To deal with the flux of ever-changing conditions and find some stability, the body creates habits, which are energy efficient, especially for your brain. They keep you safe, offer the illusion of some control, free up your survival-scanning mode for more creative pursuits, allow some respite for the planning part of your brain, and make multitasking possible. So, habits contribute in a big way to your own evolutionary journey—you don't want to rid your life of predictability. Because they are automatic, you may be unaware of some of them because they are so embedded in your life. Watch someone constantly grooming their new beard, or incessantly checking their phone for updates on their social media feed. A habit can also be a self-created prison of sorts: you take refuge in old habits of mind and body that may not be skillful, just because they feel comfortable—an old shoe that fits well, but may not be in your best interest to wear as you explore new territory.

Every insight in this book is useless unless you try it on, make it your own, and experience something tangible and visible as a result. I invite you to subject every appealing concept to the mortar and pestle of living it in your daily life, to really see if it provides the transformative spice you are looking for. Practice makes permanent, not perfect! Be aware that knowledge alone does not alter behavior. In order to manifest your dreams in the world, or to shift internally, it is essential that you understand and engage with the change process. A large portion of your development is to continually identify those habits of thinking and being which do not serve you. Then prioritize: what's on tap, what's on top, what really needs to be dealt with and is asking for your skillful attention? That is how you cultivate your own garden, and become more effective in the world.

Never underestimate your propensity to deceive yourself. Perhaps you are getting feedback that your anger is messing things up, or your drug and alcohol use or some other addiction is contributing to your falling apart. Maybe you have the same repetitive expectation about a person or situation, and are continually disappointed. If you keep doing what you've always done, you will keep getting what you've always received. If you want a divergent result, do something different. For things to change, *you* have to change. When you connect a change or intention to your purpose – and the deeply held values that guide you – it has more power. In my own life, I have come to appreciate that skillful habits create a positive life trajectory, and any successful change process embraces these six elements: awareness, belief, commitment, deeds, evaluation and focus. They are just an expanded look at the traditional "plan, do and review." Intentions create specific results in the outer world: I want to run a seven-minute mile, or make a CD of my own music. Habits are the inner changes that support achieving your intentions: regular exercise or daily practice writing and playing songs. Life's unfolding includes both letting go of whatever unskillful habits weigh you down, and manifesting what you want through creating intentions. Both are dependent on this change progression:

Awareness: Since awareness creates choice, get as clear as possible about exactly what it is you want to shift. Treat each guest honorably – all the voices in your head that offer suggestions– as a messenger from your inner wisdom. This requires some contemplation about what is, and is not, working for you in your life. Time alone and journaling can be of tremendous assistance in elucidating one prioritized focus, and articulating it in one sentence, which expresses it in positive and exciting terms. Use the

SMART mnemonic: **S**pecific, **M**easurable, **A**ttainable, **R**elevant and **T**ime bound. You thus put energy into the new, allowing the old to drop away of its own accord.

Beliefs: The door to your cage is always open, but doubt can cripple the actions required for the next stage of liberation. You must believe the desired change is possible. What is it about your thinking that creates walls to what you want? You become what you think about! Fill your mind with the positive results as if you have already achieved them. This is done through regularly visualizing and embodying all the good sensations and feelings of the desired outcome.

Commitment: Yes is acceptance, yes is willing, yes is trust, yes is what unites and transcends. Rather than repress the "no," simply ignore it. Fear is always present with change. It lives in the chasm between the known and unknown, the actual and possible, where you are and where you are going. To move through it you must know it, name it, and befriend it. Wholehearted commitment allows you to love the practice and process, as much as the end product or goal. You marshal the preparations needed for action, and enlist the support of others, by sharing the details with positive, supportive friends.

Do it: Clear intent and positive action feed off each other in an uplifting spiral. The ancient wisdom of "the path is formed by walking on it" acknowledges that when you do something every day to create the desired shift, you gather momentum. What gets stimulated gets enhanced, what gets rewarded gets done. Resistance often manifests as negative *mindtalk*, self-defeating behaviors, avoidance and procrastination. The key here is to be in no resistance to your resistance! À la Star Trek, resistance is futile! Just observe it without judgment, honor it as a very important teacher. Choose "yes" to what nurtures, drop the "should," embrace your willingness to tolerate frustration and postpone some gratifications because of your commitment. Just keep renewing your patience, and engage every day with the desired habit or intention.

Evaluate: Ever watch a baby learning to walk? They fail more than succeed, but get lots of positive encouragement and keep fine-tuning until they get the flow right. So think baby steps, as you move from breakdown to breakthrough to breakout. Every setback is a setup for the comeback. Things going wrong are just part of the process. Examine the *how*, rather than the *why*, of the breakdown. *Why* questions just keep you stuck: I didn't exercise because I didn't have time. *How* queries move you toward a solution, because they direct you to a specific correctable choice point: how that happened was I overscheduled my afternoon. Look for feedback –the breakfast of champions – as the doorway to what needs to shift: awareness, acceptance then refined action. Be consistently persistent, and celebrate the little wins as habits evolve.

Focus: Each day brings many competing desires.

Not to mention the constant background patter, and the endless parade of should and have-to-dos. Whether you are creating a habit change, or manifesting an intention, you only have so much time and energy. Focus is ongoing engagement with a desired outcome until it manifests. It understands the superiority of attention over the will as the ultimate tool of self-transformation. It is about *skillpower* rather than willpower. Like an airplane that must keep correcting its course as it goes, you can refocus on what needs doing to make forward progress.

Now Go Deeper
Choose a new habit or intention and declare it using the SMART format. How does it make you feel to articulate the desired change so clearly?

The ABCDEF process is the mechanism by which you take what begins merely as a thought, and transform it into a new habit, or a manifested intention. I use the term "inner wheel" shift for habits because they reflect an internal process of personal *behavioral* change; intentions are the "outer wheel" because they involve producing a tangible *physical* result—a new demonstrable skill or created object. Manifesting intentions and creating empowering habits help you to live your purpose, and fulfill your needs and wants. Over and over in my own life, I have discovered that whenever things are not manifesting in the outer world, it usually means I need to shift focus to the inner wheel. The Rolling Stones got it partially right: You can't always get what you want, but if you try sometime, you find you get what you need. Consider this instead: You can't get *everything* you want, but conscious intention and habit change will help you manifest those deep desires that positively influence your evolving path of self-realization. If the question is what are you waiting for, then the answer is the rest of your life, and it unfolds with each habit you embody that supports your most essential values.

XVIII

ALTERED CONSCIOUSNESS

When do you feel really alive? This sensation usually arises when you are centered in your purpose, fulfilling some deep desires, enjoying your life, and making progress in letting go of those habits and perspectives that no longer serve you. All of this forward motion can be attained without the high-risk activity of experimenting with substances. The hypocrisy of "just say no" makes some drugs illegal, stigmatized and dangerous, while others, such as alcohol, tobacco, and increasingly, marijuana, get a free ride—despite having clear adverse health consequences. By all means, avoid alcohol and other drugs as much as possible while your brain is having its growth spurt, from ages 14 through 18. Beyond that timeframe, just say maybe. And never take anything with uncertain purity, or without having some sense of what you might experience. Taking something a stranger offers you at a party, concert, or a rave is not intelligent! Some subliminal and sublime substances do have the potential to alter your perceptions, and help you clearly see what needs to shift in your life. And many people who experiment will experience more damage and destruction than growth and insight.

What are you seeking when you use drugs? The alleviation of physical or emotional pain is one obvious answer; inducing euphoria for pleasure and escape from everyday tedium are others. Many people use recreational drugs to self-medicate anxiety, depression or other mood disorders, seeking only to flee through an easy portal to oblivion. Many youth just do it because it shows up in their sphere, and seems like it might be fun to try. Narcotics or psychedelics, stupefaction or insight, drugs offer many diverse avenues for exploration. It is completely normal to want to change the channel of awareness. You do this all the time with music, workouts, lovemaking, and even savoring a great meal. Substances are just an easy way to open that door. You live in a culture that encourages medication and pharmaceuticals. But it's in your best interest to learn lots of ways to alter consciousness and not rely on one mode. Play with meditation, mindfulness or visualization as modalities to dissipate physical pain. Get those communication skills developed so that alcohol is not needed as a social lubricant. Experiment with breathing exercises, Qigong, mudras, acupressure points, and other ways to produce an energy lift, rather than nicotine or caffeine. Even altering your body posture to more of a comfortable power stance – the head up-chest out-hands on hips pose – has been shown to increase confidence building testosterone, and lower stress related cortisol levels. Our minds change our bodies, and our bodies change our minds.

Now Go Deeper
Draw, collage, sculpt or write down all the ways you already enjoy changing the channel of your consciousness. What new avenues hold some allure?

Reality vastly exceeds your awareness of it. Your brain reduces and filters the amount of stimuli it receives from the world to a manageable level in order to promote survival. Your mind tunes out the cross talk of information from the more expansive conscious *oneflow* of everything. If you slept all night as soon as it became dark, you would not know about the existence of stars, yet they are always there. Bats can "hear," dogs can smell, and dragonflies can see realities that are invisible to you because of your sensory limitations. Psychedelics, a class of drugs defined by their ability to expand consciousness, simply temporarily remove some of your brain screens. They modulate your brain's neurochemistry, altering cognition, mood, and perception of time and space. You experience a vaster mind than ordinary waking consciousness. Nothing can quite prepare you for this novel, intense collision with the present moment. Preconceived notions of reality and your own personality can scatter like stardust, as you tap into a larger well of consciousness, an expansive reframing of worldview.

Curiosity will always trump criminalization, but the idea here is not just a mystical "wow," nor the fleeting thrill of a nebulae-to-neurons funhouse. By unlocking certain serotonin receptors, psychedelics open doors to new vistas, often generating enchanted surroundings entwined with your deepest aspirations. You may feel deeply connected to self, others, and the world at large. Many report rich clarity, layer upon layer of understanding, from interacting with the world in such a different way—an onion of questioning peeling away to reveal a sparkling moment of insight cut from the cloth of time. The 1960's invitation to "turn on, tune in, and drop out," carried its share of collateral damage, including painful and confusing states mimicking psychosis. Although humans have ingested plant-based psychedelics for thousands of years, some caution is clearly advised, which means you must understand the importance of set and setting.

Set is the mindset with which you approach using a substance. If you are upset or angry and hoping the drug will calm you down, remember that alcohol and other drugs can magnify negative emotional states, and make these feelings take over. Personal problems, troubles at home, and issues you are afraid to face can all take form in unique visions that may be scary and overwhelming. So, always best – especially with hallucinogenic agents – to be in a relaxed, content, calm, centered state. Where you consume drugs definitely contributes to the reactions you will have as well. The setting includes not only physical location but also other elements – ambient light, noise and temperature – that can positively influence your experience with a drug. Avoid places where you might feel scared or threatened. Being able to leave the locale can alleviate negative reactions if they start to occur, and having an experienced guide can greatly reduce the chances of a bad trip. Turning off TV, computers, and telephones, while being outside in a safe place in nature, can also contribute to an exploration free from worry and stress, minimizing intense adverse reactions.

Being drug free is more than okay: it feels really great to not need any drugs—legal or illegal! Many people live very fulfilled lives without ever experimenting with substances. They see through the glamorous claims of advertising lies, and mostly avoid alcohol, tobacco and pot, because they are clear that the negative health effects are not worth it. They resist the peer clamor that "everyone is doing it," if it does not ring true and feel right to their own path. I hope you can avoid the toxic, destructive cycle of frequent substance use, habitually trying anything just to get high. In my experience, most substances – especially heroin, methamphetamine, and many "designer" drugs – have very few redeeming qualities in terms of expanding your awareness. Within my own circle of friends, I have too often directly experienced their addictive, enslaving damage. Others, such as *nootropics*, are at the forefront of exploring what is possible in terms of brain potential, also true for some herbal preparations, and the non-substance modalities of transcranial direct current or magnetic brain stimulation. If any drug starts becoming your best friend, the place where you often want to go first to find comfort when you are down, or to celebrate when you feel up, that is big feedback that you are not in wholesome relationship with it. Using every day, or wanting to, means you need to shift your involvement with a given substance if you really want to have a good life. We all know habitual stoners, potheads whose dreams and goals literally just go up in smoke every day.

If your mind is a product of the brain, your awareness is how you tune in: to sensations and emotions, the world around you, the energy of other beings. The more mindfully aware you become, the greater the depth of consciousness you can embody. The experience of self-transcendence has always increased my own desire to explore more of that realm. Substances allow you to glimpse the possibility of shifting out of the normal mode of verbally driven, focused, rational thinking. They teach you that the deliberate use of your attention can transform your perception of the world. How you perceive an experience determines how you feel about it. When an athlete feels pain, but associates it with health and fitness – a "no-pain, no-gain" mentality – the "bad" sensations are transformed into something positive. While psychotropic drugs, deep meditation, lucid dreaming, near death or out of body experiences can give you some good insights, real change is a more complex process. Unless such discernments are actually translated into action, every "aha!" is just a prelude to a "so what?" Cease clinging to the fixed points of your perspectives and behaviors. Demolish the familiar, and perhaps you will gather some pearls of true understanding. Read voraciously to expand the well of ideas from which you drink. Open yourself to the altered states available through being in nature, expressing your creativity, or connecting to your tribe through music, dance, and moonlight or fireside deep conversation.

XIX

CREATIVITY

Humans are classified as *Homo sapiens*, but have also been designated *Homo ludens*, or playing man. Play can be solitary or social, free or codified, competitive or cooperative, planned or spontaneous, simple or complex, physical or intellectual. Rough or gentle, strenuous or restful, its roomy improvised territory allows one to simultaneously be both spectator and actor. Lurching between regulation and abandon, order and chaos, mischief and manners, its ancient, unpredictable nature is what makes play unique from other voluntary pleasurable human activities. Children at play find the sweet abandon of *nowness* completely captivating. Although it exists for its own sake, apparently purposeless and out of the ordinary, play clearly offers a mix of physical, social, emotional, and intellectual rewards at all stages of life. It effortlessly stimulates many survival related dividends: play trains your physical skills – strength, reflexes and spatial awareness – sharpens your imagination and discovery abilities, and deepens your social capabilities, such as empathy and conflict resolution. Truly engrossing, play suspends your sense of the passage of time, and leaves you poised to play some more.

A great lie you have been fed, over and over, is that if you don't immediately show a knack or inherent talent for something, you should just give it up. The extravagant, playful creativity of childhood is soon crushed by demands of parents, education and society. Creativity is a natural human phenomenon, our single greatest survival resource, an expansive state, a flowering of your basic needs to imagine, express and manifest. Art is the ubiquitous language of symbols—universal beliefs, feelings, values, and ideas that transcend cultural and economic boundaries. No matter the medium, art transforms your relationship to the world through a genuine direct interaction, while it enlarges the space inside you as well. We put ourselves into the world, and it changes us from the inside out. The craftsmanship of long ago still reveals its secrets to those who invest the energy to explore its intricacies. From basket making to pottery, exquisite jewelry to handmade clothing, fine furniture to noble tools of the trade, musical instruments to *objets d'art*, humans in every culture have married beauty to functionality, adornment to enriching the human spirit. Creativity is not efficient, though it can be gracious and generous as it wanders around back alleys, propels you forward into the light, and dresses you in dreamy, concocted, sideways, out-of-focus thinking.

Creative individuals trust their intuitive whisperings, are willing to take risks, make mistakes, and explore the fertile soil of ambiguity. They actually enjoy pushing the boundaries of their own competence, and find pleasure in the problem itself. Such a joy, to playfully experiment with new connections, moving beyond traditional assumptions and solutions! They tend to have a high ability to fully engage their concentration, with an elevated capacity for visual imagery, generating a plethora of ideas and imaginative leaps. They often act without regard for external rewards, spontaneously autotelic and with total commitment. All of these qualities help them to see the bigger picture, even as they pay meticulous attention to small details, and seek novel opportunities for action. Do you see the parallels to playing here?

Free the suppressed fearless genius who boasts a willingness to be surprised, amazed, disappointed or perhaps frightened by the results of one's imaginative labors. Welcome the elaborate intimacy of collapsing the boundaries between your body and your creations. Jettison your boring and predictable quest for validation and self-importance, and see what purity emerges. Remember always that the greater the depths to which you are willing to plunge inside, the more precious the treasures that will appear in your hands. Open the gates for your capricious renegade musings to leap and chase the wind. Keep looking for meaning in unusual places by engaging with your strangest notions, greeting the unfamiliar with open eyes. Embrace the wildness of the visionary way. Even when you are not focused on a specific creative endeavor, it is fun to keep those creativity muscles exercised. Try out these eight ways. Each asks you to silence the inner critic, drop perfectionism, trust the process, and open your imaginative floodgates.

Astonish yourself: use beginner's mind to walk around the same old neighborhood and immerse yourself in the novelty hidden in the commonplace; scrutinize an old familiar object and discover new details you never noticed; do the same with someone's face. Pretend you are a specific animal. Shower with your eyes closed, transporting yourself completely to different water environments. Sing in a made-up language.

Brainstorm: suspend judgment, trust that quantity engenders quality, combine and improve ideas. Although usually done in a group, keep the muscle active by solitary practice. How many things can one do with a match or a paper clip?

Create with your hands: play with building, sculpting, sewing, sleight of hand, drumming, drawing, massaging, pottery.

Carry a vade mecum: a pocket sized sketchbook or notebook, to capture those random bursts of creative seeing. Pick an image or phrase that appeals and hang it where you can see it when you go to sleep and first awake—a little idea that you don't completely understand but don't want to forget about.

Mindmap or cluster: put a key idea or word in the center, then draw related spokes as thoughts, words and associations piggyback on each other. Generate connections without analysis until a useful pattern emerges.

Enter the hypnogogic state: lie horizontally in bed while sleepy. Bend your arm at the elbow and hold it up vertically. As you fall asleep, it will naturally drop, and you will be awakened with a rich but fleeting treasury of images.

Nourish chi: access the universal intelligent creative energy that is always available at any moment, just by opening yourself and being receptive; various traditions, such as martial arts, Tai Chi, Qigong and yoga, teach you how to cultivate, store and express it.

Salons: form or join a regular creative salon that enables people to allow their own voices, hands, words and deeds to become playfully cooperatively alive, as they create together in the moment. A joyous place free of both criticism and compliments, sharing creativity in myriad forms: dance, poetry, music, writings, visual arts, sculpture, or crafts.

Now Go Deeper
What creative gift is calling you to deepen your exploration of it?

You don't need to be super-talented or fortunate enough to have gotten an early start at whatever ingenious endeavor you are attempting. You just need to keep on keeping on, to muster patience, to love the eternal now of consistent, persistent practice. Embrace the inevitable plateaus, and continue to play at the edge of your own incompetence. Don't get stuck in the small stuff. When bored or restless, *shapeshift* and imbue the now with grace, efficiency and elegance. The rhythmic wanderings of clock time, sky time, bio time and cosmic time invite you to touch the source, and dance with your own life force.

I have developed a habit of setting aside time each week to nourish my wellspring of creativity. While it is important to pay attention to the crucible of my own flame, I also regularly seek out those who inspire me with their artistry of living. You might play with increasing the depth of your quirky eccentricity, and turn some social constraints upside down. Pay homage to the importance of fallow times, and the emptiness of long breaks. Moments of unburdened contemplation are essential to the creative process. Forget all you have been told that such is the stuff of self-indulgent luxury or deplorable lazy idleness. Perhaps you'll notice the exquisite choreography of clouds, the splendid jazz of birdsong, how moonlight might alter your normal perceptions. Some of the world's best ideas, art and philosophy emerged from the sparks generated in the quiet stillness of being totally attuned to the inner universe, while highly attentive to the outer world, and one's sense of belonging to it.

Make no blind obeisance to tradition, doing things because they have always been done that way. Humans might still be huddling around campfires for warmth, and reading by candlelight. Remember that the penetrating beauty of artistry can be a form of resistance, an impetus for necessary social change. Suffer for art only to the extent necessary; not every artist need be dysfunctional or crazy. Try not to plan more than you produce, and always take criticism as an invitation to grow. Please personify "first things first," and don't allow the endless stream of chores, errands, email and to-do lists sidetrack your creative output. Every to-do list needs a sidekick to-don't list: don't stress, don't obsess, don't procrastinate, don't get lost in the worry maze. For the creative artist, life is abundant and nothing is insignificant or unimportant. Break the spell of "I can't!" Discover your unique brilliance, that arena where you produce positive results effortlessly, generate energy easily, and experience deep creative fulfillment and satisfaction.

XX

HAPPINESS AND FREEDOM

There are some goals that you cannot pursue directly. When you chase them intensely, they only flee from you. The hunt spooks the prey. While you are *trying* to be happy, the part of your brain that is actively exerting itself stands in the way of the spaciousness of being joyful. It's a bit like attempting to repair a bicycle while you are riding it. Like the other basic emotions, happiness exists along a continuum, from contentment and delight to elation and ecstasy, each emanating a deeply felt, complete sense that all is well. The body is relaxed but energized, the heart at peace, the mind engaged yet serene, a state where nothing needs to be changed. Short-term sensual pleasure is just that—the thrill of the new gizmo before it inevitably breaks down, the exquisite flavors of a finely cooked meal, that great massage. Such temporary feelings of fulfillment, although they do not last, can still be appreciated for the delight they bring! It's a bit insane to crave permanent happiness when everything is constantly changing: bodies get sick and age, cherished objects get damaged or lost, sensual delights fade, and relationships encounter stormy seas.

How much happiness are you willing to allow in your life? Try it: anytime you smile, laugh, dance or sing, you improve your brain chemistry, and thus invite gladness in, without directly seeking its presence. Happiness lives in the most ordinary of moments, sometimes appearing as unexpected stubborn joy in the face of ruthless difficulties. While you can't really plan for moments of rapture, don't try to prevent them either. Life's tragic impermanence and simultaneous vibrancy meet in the center of the fragility of the present moment. The key to happiness is to enjoy it when it arises, and cease seeking it when it does not. If you want exactly what you have, then there is no lock that needs to be opened.

You have a singular capacity for self-liberation, and incongruously, you are the architect of your own suffering. Explore the house of detention you have built. I have watched my own fears generate certain habits and patterns that kept me craving and judging—bars of the cage of illusions in which I was trapped, even though the door to freedom was wide open. As they can, each person is busily constructing larger, more comfortable, confining cells. Wandering, scurrying, aimlessly searching for a morsel of meaning in a vast prison of empty promises. I still sometimes forget that what I seek lives within, lost dream treasures hiding in the attic, priceless purpose in the basement of my discarded selves. Are you just polishing the prison bars, playing victim, rather than doing the arduous work of transforming unskillful conditioning?

The incessant demands of how you *should* behave, *should* be feeling, or *should* be doing are also not likely to fill you with rapture. Who wants to live in should land, trapped by the constant commands of self or others? Yet every day most of us allow a pile of them to smother our curiosity, creativity and contentment. Remodel each should into a want, or drop it. Learn to stop the war within by inviting your inner sage to take the podium when the disparaging chorus of the inner critic gets too loud. These letters have been encouraging you to lower the volume on your *yama yama* considerations, to handle your own crazy *ya ya* – all the mental negative chatter you let run loose – and reject those specific social lies and cultural norms that only further confine you. Every moment of awareness is a hammer stroke on the chain of your conditioning.

How to be a joyful participant in a world full of sorrows? Famine, wars, global disasters, climate change, and the seemingly endless everyday violence between humans can certainly make you feel powerless, insignificant, and chip away at your vitality and *joie de vivre*. Your own incredible privilege can sometimes seem a burden, given the suffering and inequities visible everywhere. Remember that

163

many in the world manage to create cheerfulness and laughter despite deprivation, danger, and generally horrible external circumstances— they can serve as role models for you. Poverty, strife and struggle do not always equate with misfortune and lack; they may beget radiant genius and beauty, and often inspire the best in people. When the horrors in the world threaten to overwhelm, create the space that allows you to grieve, nurture and replenish yourself. Keep your heart open and light. Persist in doing whatever you can to make the world a better place, starting with yourself and your immediate environs—some measure of happiness will always arise from that.

Freedom is straightforward but not simple. Freedom *from* and freedom *to* are just two sides of the awareness coin. As you drop family baggage and unskillful patterns and habits, you will easily begin to experience more liberation. Freedom welcomes all the diversity of your inner experience—including strange desires, contradictory impulses and emerging competence. It is an upward spiral movement in which you continually let go of past limitations, doubts and illusions. Freedom arises more and more as you build capacity to pause between stimulus and response. The beliefs and thoughts in your head and heart are what keep you in jail. Liberation demands that you be thankful for every moment of living. Freedom expands directly to your capacity to not take yourself, or whatever marks you make in the world, too seriously.

Happiness and freedom are less a matter of getting what you want than of wanting what you have. Most people have some idea of what makes them feel good. Usually it involves the word *more*: more money, more time with family, more travel or exciting experiences. Garages and closets full of unused stuff, once so ardently desired for their temporary mood elevation, now lie in silent testimony to your own drone of dissatisfaction and endless drive for more. How much of your today is rooted in being present and appreciative? Living in gratitude is the foundation of both happiness and freedom, the substrate that binds all the connections you have: with yourself, those close to you, strangers, and the planet.

All around you, the cosmic cycles of giving and receiving create a circle of thanks in which you partake through thoughts, words and actions. Observe your normal response to the commonplace daily query of "how are you?" Perhaps you embellish your negativity with a clever ditty that you are not complaining, just explaining. Maybe you actually tell the truth rather than the socially acceptable "okay," or equally closed "fine." Rarely does one hear a response filled with an attitude of gratitude.

Now Go Deeper
Create frequent "moments of appreciation" breaks throughout the day. There is always, always something for which to be grateful.

The infinity sign is the best representation of the relationship between happiness and freedom. They are intimately entwined, and distinct states of being, both standard mammalian issue. Interdependent, they develop simultaneously, and are often expressed spontaneously. They each are *sine qua* non for the other's existence, a vast spaciousness of vital life energy, generated from inside you. You can regularly tend the garden in which abiding happiness and freedom are likely to arise. Practicing loving kindness and compassion – forms of complete generosity without the relative notions of giving and receiving – creates a fearless openness without territorial limitations. A quivering or tenderness of the heart, compassion is a feeling of closeness and sense of responsibility based on the realization that we all have similar desires to want happiness and overcome suffering. Cultivate sympathetic joy, which teaches you to celebrate the successes and happiness of others, rather than being jealous or envious. Allow equanimity to blossom— really a profound form of acceptance that understands suffering can be transformational. Whatever is happening is okay because it *is* what is happening. Utilize your state of conscious awareness for the benefit of life itself, rather than solely for personal gain. You match your breathing with the world's tumultuous sighs. May *I* be happy, peaceful and free, transforms to may *all* beings be happy, peaceful and free.

When you take a few moments at the beginning of your day to breathe in appreciation for all the good-ness in your life, and breathe out compassion for those suffering, you honor not only the people who help you survive, but also the animal, insect and plant kingdoms, without which your precious life could not exist. Long-term consistent behavior alters the baseline function of the brain. Appreciation is powerful because it is a conscious choice that, over time, alters your perception and raises your default levels of happiness and freedom. While external circumstances may influence the ease of slipping into these states, ultimately they are generated from within. The only way to stabilize them is to spend more time in them, held in their embrace, surrendering to their currents. Invite the inner glow of gratitude to fill you throughout the day, simply by switching your attention into acceptance, appreciation, awe, or amusement.

XXI

SPIRITUALITY

Have you rejected the religion of your parents? Is the idea of spiritualty not important or even on your radar? If you encountered an abundance of hypocritical phony holy, it may be difficult to even relate to the term at all. Perhaps some basic values guide your life, without invoking any divine assistance. Or it is also possible you still follow your family's footsteps, experiencing some level of connection between religious ideas and your daily existence. Think of spirituality as a personal journey, while religion is an organizational roadmap. Sometimes they cross and overlap, and while they can support each other, often one can be a barrier to the other. Religion can be narrow, exclusive, bigoted and replete with prejudice, a cloak you can wear or discard depending on what circumstances dictate. Spirituality has no bounds, while religion tends to be full of constraints. The great societal lie is the oft-expressed certainty that heaven and hell are other than here on earth, and that you must embrace a religious belief in a god—often one who monitors your every thought and action, and will punish or reward you for them. The notion that the purpose of life is to suffer, and if we do it well, then we are rewarded in heaven, never quite rang true for me. Please don't blindly accept what traditions, books, or even teachers say you should; believe only if it resonates in the inner altar of your heart, and the investigation of your own life.

The spiritual quest is something akin to going to a flea market. Many vendors will claim they have what you need. The way will be filled with an array of superficial junk, requiring sifting through to find something meaningful. I hold dearly the positive values of the religion in which I was raised, and try to practice them—just without the churchgoing trappings and interpretations. And I have forged a number of daily, weekly, monthly, seasonal, and yearly practices that put those principles into action. From a life-honoring altar in my home, to daily gratitude and affirmation routines, monthly fasting to solstice celebrations, and visiting sacred outdoor locales, I strive to keep my spiritual flame burning. "Vast sky does not hinder white clouds coming and going," is the container in which I try to dissolve my mood storms and the daily wreckage of things falling apart. I love surrounding myself in blue healing light as I do my physical workouts each week. Simple everyday acts can become imbued with spiritual presence through the gift of your loving attention and conscious connection to the greater whole. Spirituality is an active force arising from your best moments. Perhaps you have already experienced *illuminexus*: where you are now able to live what previously were only insights from peak (peek) experiences.

Now Go Deeper
What regular spiritual practices serve your wellbeing and development?

There is an alternative, diverse, spiritual sensibility that views the matrix of matter as an intelligent conscious force, an update of ancient animist concepts. "God" is everywhere in everything. Spirit is all that is. Soul is a unique wave, an individual encapsulated portion, in the universal ocean of spirit. Soul is everything that pulls you down, grounds you in desire, passion, the vitality of life; spirit is all that lifts one, awareness and higher consciousness. Soul and spirit both live within you, and healing into wholeness is breaking the illusion that they are separate. Being a good animal and having higher awareness – individual ego and cosmic oneness – serve you for survival and evolution. The goal is not "no self," but rather the freedom to experience life beyond the bounds of the self. Transcendent phenomena always surpass the container of words and your confined perceptions. Think of consciousness as a vast field of information, and your individual awareness is only a small part of it.

The self is the hub of cognition, perception, emotion and behavior, the central train station that connects these disparate experiences. The sense of self – the thinker behind the thoughts, that which is aware it is aware – is maintained by autobiographical memories. The small self of your ego perhaps developed as an early repetitive set of neural pathways, defining and stabilizing certain patterns of perception. It is a construct formed by your brain to integrate experiences and provide some cohesive psychological continuity. In fact, you have many "selves" rather than a unified, integrated one. There is the you that desires, the you that hides, the you that helps, the you that hinders, the you that doesn't have a clue about the big universe of what it doesn't know. "You" is just a seed of awareness that will grow, blossom and offer its fruits to the world. This is its inherent nature: to survive, learn lessons, enjoy the experience of being in a body, and connecting with and being of service to other travelers it encounters along the way.

For me, the essence of spirituality is connection to the universe and this marvelous planet, with its myriad life forms, impossibly small and expansively large. This includes you and me, and other sentient beings, throughout all the twists and turns of our unique, evolutionary, revelatory, transformative, individual journeys. Slow down enough to participate in these common, natural *unfoldings*—dusk and dawn with their twilight yearnings, sunset and sunrise, watching the stars emerge and wink away, moonrise and moonset, the turning of the seasons. This creates a reverence for the ordinary. It honors the awe-inspiring mystery, the beauty and bounty of the world around you—and the world seems enough, you are enough, and life's blessings are abundant and enough. When you connect to these rhythms, many of the qualities discussed in these letters arise, naturally and profoundly. Freedom, happiness, peace, and acceptance are all nurtured by the welcoming spaciousness and ordinary magic of the natural world. Beyond philosophical concepts, scientific proof, or religious trappings, you can experience the truth of this directly.

Up to your neck in the here and now, you gradually realize how interconnected absolutely everything is. The clothes on your back, the remains of supper on your plate, and the roof over your head were all fabricated, grown or created through the interdependent interactions of the biosphere and its inhabitants. Think about the common utensils that make storing, preparing, serving and eating the abundance and variety of life-giving foods you enjoy every day. The myriad tools available to modern man, which enable you to care for your surroundings, blaze the trail of your own creativity, and be safe and comfortable as you explore primitive parts of the planet. Everything from musical instruments and art supplies, to backpacking gear, hammers and vacuum cleaners, is readily available. And yes, the amazing universe of digital everything, the emerging Internet of Things, replete with the techno wizardry of smartphones; the incredible capacity for instant information, the endless streams of entertainment, and the invisible mojo of the tiny computer chips that make it all possible. As you enter an age of wearable exoskeletons, augmented and virtual realities, robotic surgery and self-drive cars, never lose touch with the basics of enduring that mankind has only recently taken for granted on such a large scale. Absolutely everything is celestial sunlight and starlight embodied. All life matters and everything belongs.

Some people just get tired of living, but scared of dying. If you consider how most humans would like to die, it is to be pain-free, aware, and enjoying what is happening—the same way one aspires to live. Both life and death dance on a razor wire of uncertainty, to the music of lamentation and celebration, filled with passion and pathos. Samurai woke up each morning refreshed by meditative thoughts of their own death, because it marvelously focused them on living. Seems ridiculous that on your deathbed, you might long to hold on, singing some sort of nostalgic "I want to go back" tune. Better to dive with glee into that numinous unknown, than regress into a whimper. What lessons can you take from the death of someone close to you, to enhance your own life? Beyond the inevitable emotional turmoil, is their passing a form of wake-up call for you—if not now, when? You may have too much youthful vigor in you to even speak of death. Yet in the secret chapel of the heart, you face the reality of your existence—how cosmically insignificant it is, but all-important to you. No one knows what occurs with death—not religious leaders, theologians, agnostics, nor atheists. But it does not matter, because life is eternal in this very moment. *Memento mori* are artistic or symbolic reminders of your mortality. Try carrying one around as a spiritual practice, and see if it reminds you to embrace life more fully. Death is the ultimate strip search, demanding that you fully reveal what you most love about being alive.

PARTING THOUGHTS

Life is richly complex and surprisingly simple, a marvelous voyage of increasing awareness. You are still learning some of the basics of conscious, empowered masculinity, so that you may take your place as a citizen of this universe. Fall into your own beauty as you embrace the tasks of life, profound and small. Wake up, grow up, and show up! Be aware of the higher reality while dealing with ordinary reality. Yes, you have been hurt and wounded by others, and the vicissitudes of life in the past. Struggle and strife often beget great beauty. Liberation comes in many flavors, and is born of experience and paying attention, more than just accumulating esoteric knowledge. You don't get to the light by the endless exploration of the dark. Engage your creative vandalism as you explore the labyrinth of your life. Be patient with shedding your unwanted traits as you navigate your destiny through fields of possibility, haunted by the mistakes you've made and those you will eventually encounter— make large monuments to your limitations. Knowledge alone does not change behavior. It must be forged in the fires of everyday existence.

Scars point to the depth of your experience, the strength of your survival, and life's lessons learned. Some people forever delay in taking action. Only at the end, do they realize their life has happened while they were waiting for it to start. Forget *Carpe Mañana!* Every man knows the bittersweet ache of regret. Embrace the delicious, lovely, complicated mess of your real life. Drop self-torment and release shame through the gradual catharsis of loving and accepting yourself. Be disturbed by your own nostalgia and desire. Cultivate robust values—rafts of absolutism on mutable seas, carrying open empty baskets filled with your own potentiality. The sense of being imprisoned by your own doubts, heavy illusions and self told lies, will dissipate when you find the sky beneath the earth. Savor the moments of luminous flow.

Seek out pleasures that money can't buy, and corporations can't command. If you're just going to do what society demands for the next fifty years, then at least request more interesting marching orders. Don't surrender your vivacious style to the dungeons of mediocrity by being a slave to convention. Humans have survived millennia of innovation, industrialization and desolation—birth, destruction and renewal seem to be our collective destiny. Always bear witness to your own truth, distilled from contemplative excursions into forbidden inner landscapes. The shifting sands of your journey can stimulate your quirky curiosity, and soften your protracted struggles. The human penchant for order, in the face of our individual ability to consistently create mess and drama, only makes us more resilient. Feel your kinship with the world. Always remember you are just one animate design among millions of other life forms sharing this planet.

Life continually asks you to let go—grieving, forgiving, and being comfortable with uncertainty. And it also requests that you bring forth—intending, creating, and being a force for good in the world. Believe in the person you want to become, the deep currents of your own life that you are stalking. Help yourself do what is yours to do. Fashion each day into a personal masterpiece. Shift your focus from what's holding you back, to what propels you forward. What are you still in denial about in your life? Taste things about yourself that you have ignored. Enjoy the lure of becoming. We are all shaped by what we choose and what we refuse. The old ways within you must die before the new perspectives can permeate your life.

I ask you to please accept the uneasy tender and troubled truce between your different deep desires – stop the war within – and hope you find the sweet spot where service and personal fulfillment coexist. Taking care of every aspect of who you are is part of your mission. Don't listen to those voices that label the science of selfishness as wrong. In order to be there for others, you must first be mindful of your own physical, emotional, mental, and spiritual wellbeing. Love is always the answer, no matter the question. Life may appear to betray you, but love will always keep its promise, and carry you forth into a far away unfathomable future. Let life seduce you. Abide in its mysteries. Do not gloss over the difficulty of leading a life of awareness. It is my sincere hope that reading these letters will ignite the fire of your own presence in your life journey. Each one holds a mirror in front of your face, and assists you to polish it. May you continue to discover, create, inspire and heal!

Sound byte pearls to keep in your consciousness pocket:
1. Question everything until you discover what resonates as true.
2. Always choose a conversation that empowers.
3. Energy follows attention. Awareness creates choice.
4. You are as sick as you are secret.
5. All feelings are okay. All behaviors are not.
6. Regularly flush the trapped anger of resentments.
7. Anything can happen at any time. Chronic anxiety is simply stuck fear.
8. Pain is inevitable, but suffering is optional. Empathy understands feelings, while compassion comprehends needs.

9. Forgiveness is a gift you give yourself. Find the ease within the effort.

10. You have to do it yourself, and you need not do it alone.

11. The gifts of sensual and sexual pleasure your body offers are exquisite.

12. Responsibility is to be taken, not assigned.

13. Give your children the present of your pre-sense.

14. Needs and desires are entirely different beasts.

15. Money is a good slave but a poor master. Everyone needs a center and an edge.

16. Respond to uncertainty with curiosity and openness, rather than fear and withdrawal. Wire it up so you always win.

17. With skillpower rather than willpower, the door to your cage is always open.

18. Honor the drive to change the channel of awareness. Find many ways to do that.

19. Love the eternal now of consistent, persistent practice.

20. Breathe in appreciation for all the good-ness in your life, and breathe out compassion for those suffering.

21. Vast sky does not hinder white clouds coming and going.

ABOUT THE AUTHOR

Victor was trained as a Pediatrician, and worked as an attending physician, teaching medical students in a Children's Emergency Room in New York City's Spanish Harlem. He also had a small private practice of babies born at home in the city. At age thirty, he embraced uncertainty and moved to Santa Fe, where he built his own home, raised two wonderful daughters, and fashioned a career in Public Health. In 1984, he began a journey to explore the different facets of conscious manhood. He saw clearly how common male belief systems were destructive to one's own health, and generated tremendous adverse impacts on families and communities. His own dedication to shifting that reality led to years of working on violence prevention issues, founding New Mexico Men's Wellness, and helping to organize large men's gatherings—seven a year are ongoing and firmly established. He is an avid practitioner of Aikido, a Japanese martial art that accepts the energy of the attack in order to transform it, and enjoys hunting elk on horseback each fall with a muzzleloader. Traveling the world continues to deeply expand his perspectives of the healthy masculine. Being in a men's support group for over thirty years, and his ongoing endless self-reflections, led him to craft this collection of Letters To A Young Man—a work of the heart, part of the joy of service and giving to others.

Please contact Victor at myheartsongs.org.

Item	Cost	Quantity

MASCULINE WISDOM
Book and 40 Card set $27   _____
WORLDWORDS: Global Reflections
to Awaken the Spirit $15   _____
LETTERS TO A YOUNG MAN
IN SEARCH OF HIMSELF $12   _____

Please add $3 per item shipping charges.
No shipping charges on orders of $100 or more.

Total Amount of purchases: _____
Shipping charges: _____
Total Amount Due _____

To order, please visit our website. myheartsongs.org
Or email: victor@myheartsongs.org

Part of the profits is donated to community groups
assisting men and veterans.